BY CLARK STRAND

Waking Up to the Dark

Waking the Buddha

How to Believe in God

Meditation Without Gurus

Seeds from a Birch Tree

BY PERDITA FINN

The Time Flyers series

The Reluctant Psychic by Suzan Saxman, with Perdita Finn

THE WAY *of* THE ROSE

THE WAY *of* THE ROSE

The Radical Path of the Divine Feminine Hidden in the Rosary

CLARK STRAND &
PERDITA FINN

Illustrations by Will Lytle

SPIEGEL & GRAU / NEW YORK

Published in the United States by Spiegel & Grau, an imprint of
Random House, a division of Penguin Random House LLC, New York.

Spiegel & Grau and colophon is a registered trademark of
Penguin Random House LLC.

LIBRARY OF CONGRESS CATALOGING-IN-PUBLICATION DATA
Names: Strand, Clark, author.
Title: The way of the rose: the radical path of the divine feminine
hidden in the rosary / by Clark Strand and Perdita Finn.
Description: First Edition. | New York: Spiegel & Grau, 2019. |
Includes bibliographical references.
Identifiers: LCCN 2019001434 | ISBN 9780812988956 (alk. paper) |
ISBN 9780812988970 (ebook: alk. paper)
Subjects: LCSH: Mary, Blessed Virgin, Saint—Apparitions and
miracles. | Mary, Blessed Virgin, Saint—Devotion to. | Mysteries of
the Rosary.
Classification: LCC BT650.S765 2019 | DDC 242/.74—dc23
LC record available at https://lccn.loc.gov/2019001434

Printed in the United States on acid-free paper

spiegelandgrau.com
randomhousebooks.com

2 4 6 8 9 7 5 3

Book design by Victoria Wong

To all our rosary friends
near and far, present and past,
living and dead,
this book is lovingly dedicated

A Word Before Reading

The Way of the Rose may be a book about the rosary, but it is not a Catholic book. Its authors are not affiliated with any religious institution. This is a book about one of the world's oldest living spiritual devotions and the Earth wisdom it still holds for those willing to reclaim it.

Contents

THE WAY
of THE ROSE

PROLOGUE

The Sign of the Goddess

THE ROSARY IS ONE OF THE MOST READILY IDENTIFIED symbols of Catholic faith—one that would seem to represent all that is most pious and conventional about Christian doctrine. Yet, hold a rosary from the loop so that the beads form a circle with the cross hanging down and it effortlessly reveals the first of its many secrets: The rosary forms the symbol for woman—a symbol that is far older than Christianity.

The word *rosary* refers to the garlands that were traditionally woven from roses and offered to the Virgin Mary in the springtime. But long before Mary, those same garlands were made as offerings to other goddesses by many other names. Roses were offered to Venus, the Roman goddess of love and fertility, whose emblem was also a circle with a cross pendant. Before that, they were offered to Isis, the Great Mother of the ancient Mediterranean world. In Egyptian images created thousands of years before the Gospels, Isis holds an ankh, the hieroglyph for Life and a variation on the same familiar symbol—an oval with a cross dangling from it that looks exactly like a rosary.

The first mention of a rosary-like devotion is over five thousand years old and refers to a *japamala*, which in Sanskrit means "muttering garland." Like the word *rosary*, *mala* originally referred not to a circle of beads but to a sacred circle of flowers. Early on, men and women simply wove their chaplets of roses for the Goddess. Later, they entwined prayers and mantras with those flowers, eventually stringing beads into a circle to perform the same symbolic gesture. A rosary is a garland of prayers woven for the goddess.

The current form of the rosary emerged in the Middle Ages as Christianity extended its dominion across pagan Europe. People were forbidden from worshipping the Great Mother of their ancestors in any explicit way, but they were able to continue their devotion to her privately while holding on to their beads. In this way the rosary became a kind of church within the Church. Old statues of Isis nursing her baby, Horus, were refashioned as images of the Madonna and Jesus. And people continued to offer their garlands to the mother goddess every spring, even if their prayers now called that mother Mary. The rosary was a way of grafting devotion to the Virgin onto the rootstock of far older, more Earth-centered forms of goddess worship handed down from prehistoric times.

Buried in the soil of those areas of Europe where the rosary first flourished have been found hundreds of devotional figurines of the goddess that are tens of thousands of years old. Long before people recorded their histories in written records, long before they settled down to live in towns and cities, they trusted the guidance and wisdom of a Lady whose body they identified with the fertile soil beneath their feet. They knew that all things—including their own bodies—had been born from the sacred womb of that Earth Mother. Just as they knew that everything returned to her.

When medieval people called out to Mary, they knew she wasn't just the mother of Jesus, as the Church would have them believe, but their mother from the bottom of time. She was with them before the beginning and after the end. She was called the Mother of Life, the Star of the Sea, the Queen of Heaven and Earth. These were the very same words of praise their ancestors had used to address Inanna, Isis, and Venus. Still, the Church insisted that Mary was not a goddess in her own right but merely an intercessor who would plead their case before an all-powerful God. Again and again, religious authorities leveled the sacred groves of the Mother to make way for churches and cathedrals. And they forbid the old prayers and practices. But people would not give up their devotion to her. She continued to be credited with all manner of miraculous healings and interventions.

The most recent attempt to diminish Mary's power was the modernizing movement within the Catholic Church known as Vatican II. Praised for its progressive reforms, this global twentieth-century gathering of cardinals and bishops was also a stealth campaign against the Virgin Mary. The Lady's celebratory prayers were excised from the mass, her feast days were deemphasized or eliminated, her statues were removed from the main altar if not gotten rid of entirely from the church. While saying the mass in the everyday language of the congregation invited increased participation, it also encroached upon the private devotions of the mothers and grandmothers used to praying with their beads as the priests droned on and on in Latin.

After Vatican II, the rosary was enlisted in the Church's ideological battles—from the fight against Communism to the war against abortion. Promoted by priests and popes alike, "The rosary is a weapon!" became one of the most popular Catholic slogans of the day. What had once been an intimate daily devotion became a political, mostly public act intended to serve the agenda of the Church rather than the needs of ordinary individuals. The rosary fell into disuse as a private ritual, and beads that had been passed down for generations in families became ubiquitous at flea markets and junk shops.

Throughout those years the Lady herself was making appearances with greater and greater frequency—in Egypt, Japan, Bosnia, Venezuela, Rwanda, America, and countless other places around the world—almost always with the message that hard times were coming and that people should pray the rosary. But the Church ignored most of these apparitions, almost as if they hoped that by ignoring the Lady whom many people still thought of as divine in her own right, they could get her to go away.

In 1969 the world's foremost scholar on the rosary, Eithne Wilkins, herself not a Catholic, asked why the rosary hadn't spread to people of all faiths and all walks of life. She saw women claiming their power through the feminist movement and young people questioning institutional authority and thought for sure that they would turn to the rosary and the long-forgotten Way of the Mother. In her groundbreaking book, *The Rose-Garden Game*, she wrote:

> There is no reason why the comparatively simple and quite painless exercise of the rosary should not be cultivated by the doctrinally uncommitted, the artists, the intellectual worker, or whoever else interests himself in gaining freer access to that reservoir of psychic energy within . . . It has the advantage over

> more elaborate techniques that it can be learnt and cultivated without the supervision of a guru, master, or spiritual director.

And yet the "doctrinally uncommitted," whose ranks Wilkins already saw massing on the cultural horizon, turned east instead. Fed up with religion, they found in Asian meditation practices the seeming antidote to the hypocrisies of their childhood churches and synagogues. Only much later would they have to come to terms with the abuses of sexual and financial power that seemed to plague the meditation masters as often as they did the priests.

As a mystical practice, meditation has always been primarily a masculine discipline. One of the most interesting speculations on its origins suggests that it evolved from hunting behaviors—the need for radical stillness and silence, for focused awareness, and for the pinpoint readiness to act when the moment was precisely right. Bead practices, on the other hand, seem to have evolved from the gathering behaviors of women as they collected seeds and nuts and berries. If the hunter is quiet and concentrated, the gatherer is a multitasker—chatting, muttering, moving about, and communing with others. Legions of grandmothers have wrapped their rosaries around their wrists, sneaking in a prayer or two between the dishes and the laundry. Children can be tended, old people cared for, the carrots chopped for dinner, all while staying in conversation with the Lady.

Perhaps because of its association with the feminine, the rosary has often been overlooked by the spiritually adventurous. It can feel modest, dowdy, perhaps a bit tame. For this reason, it can be difficult to imagine, in the beginning, how rosary beads, humble as they are, can bring forth so much beauty, love, healing, and—

yes—so many miracles of all kinds. But they can, and they have, for as long as anyone can remember.

To the person who has never seen an oak tree, an acorn might seem only a dull brown stone. Poppy seeds look like nothing so much as flecks of grit—until they become a field of bright red flowers. The fifty-nine beads of a standard rosary rest in our open palms like a handful of seeds . . . small, hard, almost inconsequential. But the moment we take those seeds in our hands, they begin to grow.

Each of the fifty-nine chapters of the book that follows corresponds to a bead of the rosary, offering readers a guided journey through a devotion that is at once firmly rooted in the spiritual traditions of the past and yet breathtakingly radical in the way it allows us to imagine the renewal and protection of all life on Earth.

The rosary guides us on the path of the heart that takes us back to the sweetness and consolations of the Divine Mother of us all. Praying the rosary gives us a way to reclaim our devotion to that Mother, get our feet on the ground again, and find our way back to the garden of the Earth.

The rosary is a new way that is really an old way, perhaps the oldest way of all. We begin by holding this ancient symbol of the Mother of All Life in our hands.

THE PATHWAY TO THE ROSARY

Am I Not Here Who Am Your Mother?

How does an ex-Buddhist monk who isn't a Catholic, and no longer even considers himself nominally a Christian, end up praying the rosary? In the ordinary course of events, it would never have happened. But, then, these are hardly ordinary times. The rosary wasn't anywhere on my list of last-ditch efforts to make sense of a world on the brink of ruin. I'd tried everything—from meditating alone in the mountains in the middle of the night to experimenting with all manner of spiritual practices, some so obscure that the religious experts I consulted could tell me almost nothing about them. In the meantime, I struggled with the demands of raising a family, worried about the choices that Perdita and I were making as parents. Panicked about climate change and what it would mean for our children and grandchildren, I sought out experts who would tell me what to do. But it never occurred to me to pray the rosary. It's the classic fairy tale in some respects—a man undertakes a quest over many years, only to find that the thing he has been searching for was always close at hand.

After the birth of our second child, Perdita and I were struggling financially. A book I'd spent a year writing hadn't sold, mortgage and health insurance payments were due, and our bank account was practically empty. We had a Visa card, but only one hundred dollars of credit left on it, and we had no idea how long that was going to have to last. Perdita rummaged for spare change in various containers around the house one day and sent me to the cheapest grocery store, the next town over, for milk and eggs.

On the way home I drove past a small antiques shop that someone was running out of the second floor of their home. In the dormer window, just visible from the road, was a statue of a dark little woman with an expression of such unfathomable sweetness it made me pull over and stop the car. She reminded me of the statue of Kuan Yin, the Goddess of Mercy, from the temple in Upstate New York where I'd once lived as a Zen Buddhist monk—only dirtier. Dirtier . . . and more loved. Blackened over time, she looked like she'd had candles burned at her feet for at least two centuries, and possibly a lot longer. She wore a headdress with a crown and, with her head tilted slightly to one side, she gazed pensively at the sphere she held in one hand. I was pretty sure it was the world.

The antiques dealer thought she was a replica of a medieval statue of the Virgin Mary, but she didn't know for sure. I didn't know either, but I could tell she was no replica. You didn't get a patina like that from any workshop or factory. How she'd gotten to Woodstock, New York, was anyone's guess.

It was a crazy thing to do, but I just couldn't help it. I feared that if I left her in that little window overlooking the road, the next time I drove by she would be gone. I'd live out the rest of my days with that sense of a missed connection that people sometimes speak of that haunts them for the rest of their lives.

The dealer wanted a hundred dollars, so I handed her my credit card. And that was that.

When I got back to the house, Perdita was exasperated. "I send you off with a cow, and you come back with magic beans!" But her irritation was short-lived. Or maybe the Lady had already begun her magic. By the end of the day, Perdita had transformed the mantel above our fireplace into an altar, complete with an offering of wildflowers she'd picked in the backyard with the kids.

That was when I first learned that, as a small child, Perdita was always making altars to the Virgin Mary—in her room, in the hollow of a tree in the backyard, and pretty much everywhere else. There was no precedent for it in her family. Her mother was a bohemian artist, her father an atheist surgeon who'd utterly rejected his parents' pious Irish Catholicism. Perdita had never seen the inside of a church when she was a girl, but she told me that she felt protective of a small broken Mary figure that she had found as a child, the remnant from some lost Nativity scene. Now, after a lapse of three decades, she was creating an altar to Mary again. In an old chest of memorabilia, Perdita found her childhood figurine and leaned it against the statue of the medieval Queen of Heaven.

Perdita and I were not brought up with the rosary. I grew up a southern Protestant. That meant that I knew the Our Father but not the Hail Mary, God the Father but not the Mother of God. When I was eighteen, I left home, left the church, and became a Buddhist. Perdita had briefly converted to the faith of her ancestors while in college, mostly because of her commitment to social justice, but no one in the church had bothered to teach her the rosary. With her feminist leanings, there was no way that she could remain a Catholic for long in any case. Soon, she, too, became immersed in Zen meditation practice.

As parents, we were trying to raise our children as Buddhists. Perdita had started a children's program at the Zen monastery where she was a student, and I was traveling around the country teaching workshops on a simple meditation practice I'd developed that didn't require masters or gurus of any kind, including myself—which meant, of course, that it wasn't a very profitable venture.

It was on one of those teaching tours, with stops in California and New Mexico, that another Madonna unexpectedly entered my life.

Strange things happened on that trip that I couldn't begin to make sense of at the time. The tour began at a former Dominican convent in San Rafael, California, with statues of Our Lady of the Rosary everywhere. I don't recall being particularly moved by any of these, but I liked the meals in the large convent refectory, where she gazed down benignly from her perch above the tables. Inspired by their meditation teacher, Thich Nhat Hanh, these ex-Dominicans were doing their part to bring greater peace to the world by opening their home to workshops on all kinds of spirituality.

On the final morning of the ten-day retreat, I left hurriedly after breakfast to get to the airport. The former sister who drove me said we'd have plenty of time to get there, but it didn't work out that way. We ended up in a tangled mess of traffic on the expressway that left me leaping from the car on the exit ramp to make a dash on foot to the airport. I figured I'd have just enough time, if I ran, to check in and get to the gate.

My heart sank when I saw the line at the ticket desk. There was no way I would make my plane. I'd miss my connection to Taos on the once-daily single-engine flight, and that meant I would miss the large weekend retreat I was supposed to be conducting with a friend. Without the money from that retreat, I'd just break even for the trip. No loss. No gain. Two weeks away from my family, with nothing to show for it but good karma. It was the way things often went in those days. At least Perdita wouldn't be surprised.

With no alternative, I joined the line anyway. If I missed the retreat, I'd still have to book a flight back home. But then something strange happened. I suddenly felt the impulse to pray.

As near as I could recollect, I hadn't prayed in almost thirty years. I had chanted. I had meditated. I had contemplated the dead. I had invoked all kinds of protective spirits in the traditional Buddhist way. But in all that time I had not once, very simply, asked any Higher Power for help.

Maybe it was my stay in the convent amid all those holy icons and statues. Or maybe it was just the financial desperation of a tired husband who felt bad about coming home empty-handed yet again. I closed my eyes and searched for words to pray with. I could think of nothing but "Have mercy on me!" The universal prayer.

I said it once . . . twice . . . three times.

Then I felt a tap on my shoulder.

A dark, heavyset man in a uniform was standing beside me. "Are you on the connecting flight to Taos?" he asked.

For a long moment I just stared at him, blinking. Finally, I snapped out of it and stammered, "Yes! I am."

"Come quickly then," he said and motioned to the electric cart he'd arrived in seconds before. He took my ticket and stepped to the front of the line, whispering something to the agent, who glanced briefly in my direction before checking me in. Then we were off.

I said nothing to this man as we careened through the airport hallways, scattering travelers to either side, but I remember wondering if maybe he'd been a Mexico City cabdriver in some earlier incarnation. It didn't occur to me to ask how on earth he had known that, among all the people standing in line, I was the one going to Taos . . . or who had sent him to find me. I hadn't spoken to anyone at the airport. I asked my nun friend later if she had told someone there to assist me, but she hadn't. All I said when we got to the gate was "Muchas gracias!" and I was off. I was afraid to break the spell.

That sense of enchantment followed me to New Mexico, where, from the moment I set foot in Taos, I began noticing the image of a particularly captivating Mexican girl. That was the way I described her to myself. A young girl. She looked to be around sixteen or seventeen years old, and she was everywhere I went—on the dashboard of the cab that picked me up from the airstrip, on a calendar behind the woman who checked me in at my hotel, and pretty much everywhere else.

I'd find her gazing down at me from the wall of the restaurant where I'd stopped for lunch. Or I would look for souvenirs to bring back home to Perdita and the kids, and roughly one third of the items in any store would bear her image. Still restless and unable to sleep because of the altitude that first night in Taos, I stepped outside and followed a path for two miles through the desert only to find myself standing before her statue, set against the backdrop of a thousand stars.

On Sunday, wandering through town during a break in the retreat, I passed a terra-cotta plaque attached to a column dividing what appeared to be the Taos version of a townhouse from a tiny alleyway shop selling plants and flowering cacti. There she was again. It almost felt like she was following me.

An older, gray-haired woman in a suit had just emerged from the townhouse clutching a leather portfolio. Eyeglasses dangled from a chain about her neck. The thought occurred to me that she was either a professor or a real estate agent.

I pointed to the plaque as she stepped past it on the way to her car and asked, "Excuse me, do you know who this figure is? She seems to be everywhere in this town."

She put her glasses on to look up at the plaque, as if she hadn't noticed it before.

"Yes. That's La Morenita, the little brown-skinned girl."

I must have looked perplexed, because she continued. "She's the Catholic version of the Aztec Mother Goddess Tonantzin, otherwise known as Coātlaxopeuh. Say it fast three times and it sounds like the Spanish name they gave her: Guadalupe."

"She's everywhere," I repeated stupidly.

"But of course!" the woman added matter-of-factly. "She's the Virgin indigenous to this region of the Americas, after all."

And that must have concluded the matter in her mind. She smiled, opened her car door, and a moment later she was gone. A professor after all, I thought.

I stood for a few moments longer looking up at the terra-cotta relief of the young woman with her hands clasped in prayer, her body backlit by the rays of an invisible sun. It took a second to realize that someone else had come to pay respects to the Virgin, her shadow merging with mine against the wall.

Dark and round, the woman was no more than five feet tall and appeared to be about fifty—although it was hard to tell: Her hair was solid black. Her smile showed one gold tooth with a cut-out star at the center. This small woman said nothing, but a moment later she kissed three fingers and, standing on tiptoe, pressed them against the Virgin's belly, which looked slightly swollen. Of course! The girl was pregnant. I hadn't realized it before.

In decades of spiritual wandering, in and out of a dozen temples, I had never witnessed anything like that one pure gesture of devotion. There was such sweetness in it. But also sadness. And a feeling of kinship . . . sisterhood perhaps. It was familiar and tender. Intimate and awe-inspiring.

And then it was over.

The woman crossed herself quickly with the fingers she'd used to touch the Virgin's belly and immediately drew back into her plant-filled little grotto of a store.

Later that afternoon, I found a book that told the story of the girl who could inspire that kind of feeling.

I read that early one morning in 1531, in an area that now lies in the northernmost part of Mexico City, an Aztec Indian named Juan Diego was on his way to church when he heard the voices of many birds singing from a nearby hilltop. The songs suddenly ended, and in the silence that followed a voice called out his name.

Juan climbed to the top of the hill and there met a beautiful young woman whose clothing shone with the radiance of the sun. She greeted him respectfully and charged him with the task of convincing the local bishop to erect a temple in her honor on that very spot. "There I will listen to the cries and lamentations of your people, in order to cure all their various pains, miseries, and sorrows."

Twice Juan tried to fulfill his task, each time without success. On the third attempt, the Virgin sent a sign for the bishop—she gave Juan an armful of roses bundled securely inside of his cloak.

When Juan unwrapped the flowers at the ecclesiastical palace, they spilled onto the floor, and there, before the eyes of the startled bishop and his attendants, was the image of the Virgin Mary miraculously imprinted upon the inner fabric of his cloak. The bishop was convinced, the temple was built, and Our Lady of Guadalupe's iconic image—along with her story—became famous throughout the world.

Today the Basilica of Our Lady of Guadalupe in Mexico City is the most popular Catholic pilgrimage site in the world, with over 20 million visitors each year—millions of them arriving for her December 12 feast day alone. The faithful begin their journeys days or weeks in advance, often carrying their statues or paintings of the "Aztec Virgin" for hundreds of miles. Why do so many make this arduous trip? Lots of people make pilgrimages to other shrines—to Lourdes or Fatima or Medjugorje—but nothing on such a scale.

Much later I would discover an essential backstory to the Guadalupe apparition that is almost never repeated within the Catholic Church.

The Virgin of Guadalupe appeared to Juan Diego during the single largest genocide in human history—20 million dead in Mexico alone in just under a hundred years. The slaughter began the very moment Columbus arrived in Hispaniola. Mothers had their children ripped from their breasts and murdered before their eyes. They saw their husbands, sons, and fathers tortured and killed, while they themselves were often raped and enslaved. It is almost impossible to imagine the magnitude of so much callous bloodlust—all justified by religious beliefs that told the conquistadors they could do no wrong, so long as they were Christian.

What happened to the natural world was no better. Entire species disappeared in a matter of decades as the rapacious appetites of the European invaders devoured everything in their path. In a pattern that would repeat itself throughout the Americas, forests were plundered, rivers polluted, great flocks eradicated, and packs of animals clubbed to death and left to rot. The ecological devastation was immediate and, in many cases, irreversible.

What violence and hatred could not destroy, disease finished off. Smallpox, measles, and other epidemics laid waste to entire populations of peoples, weakening their ability to fight off their aggressors.

Juan would have been eighteen when Columbus set foot in the Americas, in 1492. When Hernán Cortés reached Mexico, in 1519, he would have been forty-five: an Aztec Indian whose religious practice centered on Tepeyac, a hilltop where his people had long worshipped a goddess named Tonantzin, whose name meant "Mother Earth."

Tepeyac is the same hill as the one in the story, and the temple the Virgin asked to be built there would have been a replacement for the one that had been destroyed by Spanish priests less than a dozen years before. The bishop of the Guadalupe story, Juan de Zumárraga, was called Protector of the Indians because he opposed some of the more extreme forms of violence perpetrated by the conquistadors against the Aztecs. But he was an enthusiastic destroyer of Aztec culture nonetheless. Zumárraga boasted of having personally desecrated twenty thousand sacred images and razed five hundred Aztec temples to the ground. For the Mesoamerican genocide was not just the work of soldiers killing the body. It was the work of the priests to kill the soul.

Amid agonies we can hardly imagine, Our Lady appears to Juan Diego and promises him her protection. But it is such a puzzling moment in history. For she doesn't put an end to the horrors. The worst is yet to come. Her appearance means something else. Hers is the hand always held out to the hopeless during the darkest moments. "Take it," she seems to say. "Follow me, and I will ensure that your people do not perish from the face of the Earth."

That is why Guadalupe is pregnant. She appears at the end of one world yet holds the promise of another. Even the worst that human beings are capable of is no match for the life-giving Lady, who persists from one epoch to the next.

But, honestly, I did not understand any of this at the time. I finished reading most of my book on Guadalupe and marked the spot where I stopped with a little card that also bore her image. On the back of the card were her words to Juan Diego on the day she gave him the roses and told him not to worry.

Am I not here who am your Mother?
Are you not under my shadow and my protection?
Am I not your source of joy?
Are you not in the folds of my mantle,
And in the crossing of my arms?
Is there anything else that you need?

Such simple words of care and comfort. And yet they baffled me. There had been nothing in my Christian upbringing, much less in my experiences with Zen, to prepare me for an encounter with the Great Mother. Still, the words got under my skin. *Am I not here who am your Mother? Is there anything else that you need?*

I left Taos the next day with a small, hand-painted portrait of Our Lady, along with a pocketful of little Guadalupe souvenirs. When I arrived at the airport in New York, Perdita was there to greet me with our children, Sophie and Jonah. Totally out of the blue, because I hadn't realized it until that moment, I said,

"You're not going to believe this, but I have to learn how to pray the rosary."

Perdita stared at me with her mouth half open. Having the Virgin Mary on our mantel was one thing. Saying the rosary like her Irish Catholic grandmother was another. I wanted to say, "No. It's not like that."

Years later a Mexican friend would explain that when asked to state their religious affiliation, instead of identifying themselves as Catholic, many of her fellow countrymen would answer, *Soy Guadalupano!*—"I'm a follower of Guadalupe." But I couldn't explain to Perdita what I was feeling, so I didn't say anything more.

I thought she had forgotten about it, but a few weeks later, for my thirty-ninth birthday, she and the kids presented me with a rosary crafted from pink and purple plastic beads they'd found around the house.

I learned the rosary from a used book I found at the local New Age store. There was a lot of history in it, mixed with some well-meaning, if dry, theology. But the back matter included a diagram and the texts of the basic prayers. The rosary was simple enough that an average eight-year-old could learn it without any assistance. It took a day to commit it all to memory. After that I was set.

The rosary made it easier than it had ever been on the meditation cushion to enter that quiet inner space I had cultivated as a Buddhist monk. No formal posture or controlled breathing. No special instructions. It was just a matter of saying a prayer on every bead. And yet it worked. I was so surprised by this (shocked, really) that, to get to the bottom of it, I began an exhaustive study of bead traditions from religions around the world.

I discovered that as far back as anyone could remember, prayer beads had been part of nearly every religious tradition. Something about reciting prayers or mantras while holding a circle of beads seemed wedded to the spiritual impulse as surely as a baby was attached to its mother by an umbilical cord in the womb. And yet, there was good reason to believe that the very first rosaries were composed not of beads or prayers at all but of actual flowers. These would have been picked from a nearby field and woven into a garland for a goddess. When had that practice started? That was where my studies bottomed out.

It was the same for Hinduism, Buddhism, and every other bead tradition I explored. Go back far enough and you got to someone standing barefoot in the dirt with a gift of flowers for a Lady who, until recently, I hadn't even known was there. My mind could not conceive of a beadless, mantraless rosary, or even imagine what the spiritual purpose of such a long-lost "flower ritual" might have been. In a moment that seemed to reach beyond religion back to a simpler, wiser devotion to the Mother of All Life, I had witnessed a Native American woman in Taos silently touch the pregnant belly of the Virgin, but I had not yet understood what I had seen.

Later I would discover that the Divine Mother nearly always appeared on the brink of some great trial—to offer guidance and protection, to serve as a sign of hope that, in spite of everything, life will go on. Hadn't the Earth goddess resurfaced as the Virgin Mary to guide the Aztecs through their own apocalypse? That would have given me pause had I known how many apparitions there'd been of the Virgin Mary over the last century—in Portugal before the 1918 flu pandemic . . . in Bosnia before the Civil War . . . in Rwanda before the genocide.

Like many people around the turn of the millennium, I was becoming convinced that our species was approaching some final reckoning. Current projections tell us that as the result of climate change, deforestation, and other human-induced factors, over one half of all surface plant and animal species on Earth will have disappeared by century's end. Already, our oceans are mostly dead. The atrocities of the Mesoamerican genocide, horrific as they were, were only the beginning of the global ecocide currently under way.

Had I been able to wrap my mind around the full scope of the problem when I first came to the rosary, I might have followed Juan's example and entrusted myself to a Mother whose wisdom had guided all living beings on the long, sometimes dark path of evolutionary history down to the present day. But I couldn't. I was spiritually restless in those days and not likely to stick with anything for long. Soon after beginning to pray the rosary, I was distracted by Centering Prayer and Tibetan Dream Yoga, and then by dozens of other spiritual practices.

I let the rosary go. I thought it was too Catholic. I thought *Mary* was too Catholic. I had no wish to become a Catholic—or even a Christian. Years later our daughter, Sophie, would describe the rosary as a "stowaway"—a devotion to the Mother Goddess that had come down to us across the centuries hidden in the hull of the Catholic Church. Like Jack's mother in the story about the beanstalk, I tossed the handful of seeds I had been given out of the window. There, for a dozen years, they went dormant under a series of brief but intense spiritual enthusiasms. These piled up like leaves on a forest floor—waiting for the moment when Our Lady would say, "Now!"

Mother

To pray the rosary, we hold the beads in our hands . . .

OUR FIRST INSTINCT AS BABIES IS TO HOLD ON—TO A FINger, to a tress of hair, to the nipple. Medieval statues of the Madonna and Child often showed Jesus tugging at the collar of Mary's gown. Like our simian ancestors, we are born clinging to our mothers, and for the rest of our lives we will reenact that first embrace, reaching out for something to hold on to—both in moments of joy and in moments of distress. Surely that is why nearly every religion includes a tradition of using beads for prayer. When we pick up the rosary, we are like a small child reaching out to hold Our Lady's hand.

When our prehistoric ancestors followed the seasonal migrations of animals, they were in a constant state of devotion to their Mother, the Earth. Her creatures fed and clothed them. Her forests offered shelter and healing plants. Our ancestors drank from her sacred springs, cooled themselves in her rivers, and in winter her fires kept them warm. They lived in constant contact with her, their bare feet touching her body as they walked. No wonder their first artistic expressions were celebrations of that primal connection.

In caves deep in the womb of their Mother's body, these Paleolithic artists painted animals pouring forth from vulvic clefts in the rock. "This is where life comes from," they seemed to be saying. In addition to these paintings, they fashioned the earliest human images out of stone and bone and clay: all of them women's bodies. These first goddesses were endlessly varied in shape, but nearly all could fit in the palm of your hand. They were not made to stand up on their own because they were not intended for display on any altar. They were meant to be held.

Did our remote ancestors worry these figures of the Great Mother between their fingers when they couldn't find food, or when their loved ones were in peril? Did they touch them to their foreheads for good luck as they headed out to hunt? Did they keep them close during childbirth—or clutch them in their hands as they died?

We cannot know. But to dismiss these first goddesses as magical talismans is to forget that early humans also recognized their Mother in the swell of the mountains and the curve of the rivers, in the hollows of the caves and in the great trunks of the old trees. A statue made of stone was a way of acknowledging the Mother's presence in all of matter—a way of holding that presence in their hands.

This may be why people who pray the rosary today tend to keep their beads close. They wear them, carry them in their pockets, hang them from their rearview mirrors, and put them under their pillows when they sleep. Like the earliest statues of the goddess, the rosary reminds us of whom we belong to—and it reminds us that we *do* belong. The rosary is not a spiritual practice to be perfected with effort. It is a devotion that reminds us of our connection to a Mother whose very body is our planet and our home.

Mantra

For every bead of the rosary, there is a prayer . . .

MANTRA, THE REPETITION OF SACRED NAMES AND PETItions, is one of the most ancient ways of settling our minds and finding the rhythm of our heartbeats amid the noise and busyness of everyday life. Mantras get us out of abstractions and ideas, all the chatter in our heads, and back into our bodies. They unite us with the murmurs and whispers in nature, from the choruses of frogs on a spring evening to the rustling of leaves in the fall.

Every bird is identifiable by its song. When we listen to a blackbird calling to its mate, we have no idea what it is saying. Nevertheless, that call seems to express so perfectly what the blackbird is, or even what it feels. In the same way, a mantra draws from the bottommost levels of our being and our history as humans, giving voice to who we most deeply are. That is why some modern scholars have suggested that mantras may be older than language itself.

There is a joy and release that happens with repetitive prayer. Often we will find ourselves more deeply connected to our breath, more conscious of our heartbeats. When we are out and about in the world, the syllables of the mantra will fall into rhythm with our footsteps, as if the words themselves are leading us forward.

Mantras tell us where we have been, where we are, and where we are going.

For a thousand years the Hail Mary has been prayed so often, and by so many people, that it is now one of the best-known mantras in the world. The first two parts of the prayer originate in the Gospel of Luke. Like most mantras, the Hail Mary begins with a salutation to the divinity. "Hail full of grace, the Lord is with thee" is the Angel Gabriel's greeting to Mary. "Blessed art thou amongst women, and blessed is the fruit of thy womb" comes from the lips of Mary's older cousin Elizabeth. The Lady we call out to in the Hail Mary stands ready, like the Earth in spring, to bring forth life.

But the words of the final part of the mantra, "Holy Mary, Mother of God, pray for us, now and at the hour of our death," are not found anywhere in the Bible. They appear to have evolved out of the longing and memories of a people whose ancestors worshipped the Goddess—Isis, Freya, Brigid, Diana—before Christianity arrived in their part of the world. The words "Mother of God" invited her devotees to extend their imaginations beyond the limits of conventional theology. At the end of the prayer Mary is recognized not only as the Mother of All Life but also in her older incarnation, as the Queen of the Dead, who will take our bodies back into the earth when we are done with them.

Each Hail Mary follows the course of a human life from the inner darkness of the womb to the waiting darkness of the tomb . . . after which, like all mantras, it begins again. By saying it repeatedly—day after day, year after year—we rehearse the eternal drama of coming and going from this world. Like birds, we sing as the sun rises to welcome the day, and we sing, too, as night begins to fall. Gradually, our bodies learn what our minds cannot grasp: There is no time when we are separated from our Mother; there is no place we can go where we are not held in her embrace.

Mystery

For every ten beads of the rosary, there is a mystery . . .

THE ROSARY COMES TO US FROM AN ORAL TRADITION. THE medieval people who embraced it as an expression of their heartfelt devotion to the Lady did not, for the most part, know how to read. These were not people who spent much time with the Bible. In some ways they were only nominally Christian. The monks and the priests recited the 150 Psalms in Latin, along with passages from the Old and New Testaments, as part of their daily office. Meanwhile, in imitation of them, ordinary men and women started saying 150 Hail Marys on their rosary beads, telling a story that they would visualize along with their prayers. That story resembled the biblical narrative, but it was fundamentally different in its vision and message.

The priests told a story that began with Eve, a woman who disobeyed an all-powerful God, bringing evil and suffering into the world. The rosary began with Mary, a teenage girl of extraordinary courage who chose to conceive a baby without a husband, in defiance of patriarchal law. In the Gospel of Luke, Mary tells her cousin Elizabeth that giving birth to this child is a revolutionary act that will bring down the rich and elevate the poor, upending the order of civilization itself.

If the Bible concerns itself with the construction of that civilization and the reinforcement of its laws, the rosary bears witness to its collapse. Jesus's crucifixion is told through the eyes of a mother who, unable to stop the unfolding carnage, watches as the life she has brought into the world is destroyed at the hands of empire, certain of its power and justice.

In the New Testament, that misguided sense of justice reaches its fulfillment with the nightmarish final reckoning of the Book of Revelation. The rosary rejects the fiery apocalypse of the Father, replacing it instead with the Coronation of Our Lady as Queen of Heaven and Earth.

In the fifteenth century, the Church tried to impose its own narrative on the rosary, insisting that it end with the Final Judgment. But ordinary people rejected that idea. Not in any official way—it just didn't take. The rosary wasn't about instilling fear or getting people to follow the Church's rules. The story of the rosary unfolded over fifteen episodes from the life of Mary that, on an almost subliminal level, subverted the authority of the Bible itself. Those mysteries were the antidote to the existential anxiety that was inevitable in a belief system that reached its fulfillment with the end of the world.

In the mystery religions of Greece and Egypt, which preceded Christianity, the stories of the gods and goddesses offered an initiation into the secrets of the Earth. The mysteries of the rosary tell the same circular story of the natural world, in which all things come into being . . . only to die . . . only to return to life again. In an era with few books, and few who could read them, most people still hadn't been indoctrinated by the scriptures. They were, therefore, still able to read in the natural world the signs of this far older relationship to life. Those signs lay all around them—in the fields and the streams, in the mountains and the flowers, in the phases of the moon and the seasons of the sun.

The circle of mysteries that makes up the rosary weaves a spell that awakens us to the healing wisdom of the Earth itself. In nature, resurrection isn't an exceptional event. Resurrection is everywhere. This isn't a tenet of belief but an abiding truth we discover for ourselves the more time we spend inside of the mysteries. Beginnings are arbitrary, endings are temporary. This is the fundamental teaching of the rosary. The end is just another beginning when a Mother is in charge of the world.

How to Pray the Rosary

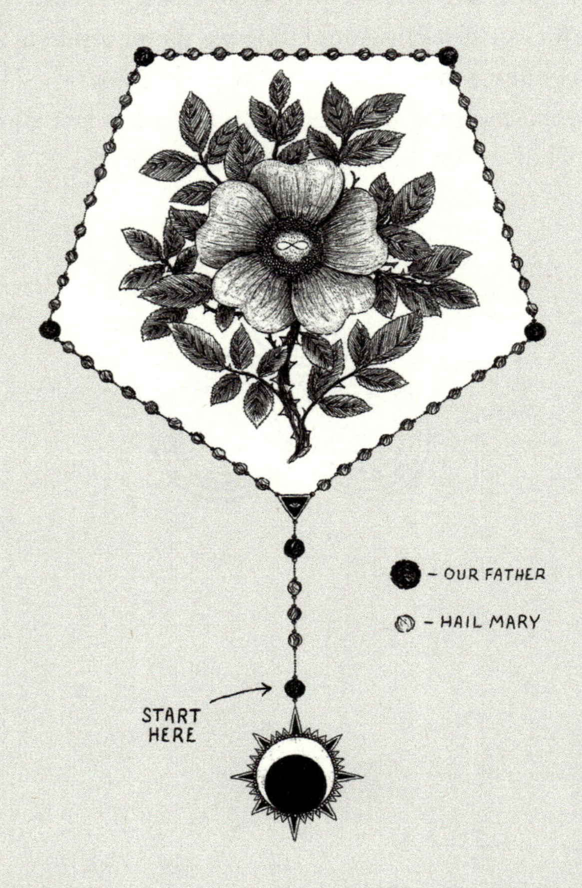

THE FIFTY-NINE-BEAD FORM OF THE ROSARY IS NOW RECognized as standard throughout the world. But it wasn't always that way. Until recent centuries, the rosary was mostly a do-it-yourself affair. You strung as many beads as you wanted onto a cord and improvised your own format for praying with them.

There were some rough guidelines to follow, of course. The rosary was Our Lady's prayer. That meant it would consist mostly of Hail Marys. In fact, for hundreds of years the rosary consisted *only* of that prayer. Eventually, the Our Father and Glory Be were added on to create the rosary we have today.

Medieval people made their own rosaries, or had them commissioned from a bead maker at a local guild. But in either case their goal was to arrive at something that worked. The same rule applies today. There is no single right way to pray the rosary. There never has been. St. Louis de Montfort summed it up quite well when he wrote, "Choose whichever method pleases you and helps you the most: You can make one up yourself if you like, as several holy people have done before now."

This does not mean that the Church hasn't long sought to control Our Lady's rose garden—to regiment it, regulate it, and set it in orderly rows. In the history of the Church, de Montfort's enlightened view is the exception and not the rule.

In the seventeenth century, the Apostles' Creed was installed like a lock on the gate to Our Lady's rose garden. This avowal of faith demanded belief in God, Jesus, heaven and hell, and—most important—the Church. Its series of *I believe*s made it clear who could and could not set foot on that sacred pathway. Only those whose beliefs were in conformity with established Christian doctrine were allowed to enter. But there was no lock originally. In the beginning, everyone was welcome. People found their way into Our Lady's presence in whatever way felt most natural. Mostly that meant just saying their prayers in a spirit of private devotion without much oversight from on high.

Finding a natural way into that garden today can be a journey in itself, especially for those who have never prayed the rosary. "Can I add the Buddhist Heart Sutra at the beginning of my rosary, or a mantra to Kali Ma at the end?" "Can I leave the word *sinners* out of the Hail Mary?" "Can I dispense with the Creed altogether and just start with the other prayers?"

The answer to such questions is invariably "Yes. Of course. Why not?"

The rosary encourages a diversity of self-expression. People make the beads their own. They decorate them with personally meaningful charms or pilgrimage medals, or with bits of ribbon from a wedding or christening. They replace the crucifix with an *ankh,* a medal of the Virgin, or a goddess figurine. As a garden, the rosary, like nature itself, has always run a bit wild. A lot of things can grow in it, and just about anything that takes root there tends to flourish on its own. Naturally. Organically. We don't have to overthink it. And we certainly don't have to worry. This isn't religion, it's permaculture. The rosary is a garden of the soul.

The rosary consists of three simple prayers, which honor
the Holy Mother, the Divine Father, and
the Eternal Return of Life.

The Hail Mary

Hail Mary, full of grace, the Lord is with thee.
Blessed art thou amongst women,
and blessed is the fruit of thy womb.
Holy Mary, Mother of God, pray for us,
now and at the hour of our death. Amen.

The Our Father

Our Father, Who art in heaven,
hallowed be Thy name;
Thy kingdom come; Thy will be done,
on earth as it is in heaven.
Give us this day our daily bread;
and forgive us our trespasses,
as we forgive those who trespass against us;
and lead us not into temptation,
but deliver us from evil. Amen.

The Glory Be

Glory be to the Father, and to the Child,
and to the Holy Mother, as it was in the beginning,
is now, and ever shall be, world without end. Amen.

The Fifteen Mysteries

To say a full rosary of 150 Hail Marys, we circle around the beads three times. In the first circle, we explore the Joyful Mysteries of conception, birth, and childhood. In the second we dwell on the Sorrowful Mysteries of suffering, death, and loss. The third circle celebrates the Glorious Mysteries of rebirth, renewal, and reunion.

Usually people commit to only one circle of mysteries each day. But there are no fixed rules or expectations. We finish one circle and begin another.

The beads of the rosary are divided into five equal sections, each with one bead for the Our Father and ten beads for the Hail Marys. These are called decades, and there is a corresponding mystery for each one. To begin each decade, we announce the mystery (see below), say the Our Father, the ten Hail Marys, and conclude with a Glory Be. Then we move on to the next decade and the next mystery. There are five mysteries for each circle.

Here are the Mysteries of the Rosary:

Joyful Mysteries

1. The Annunciation
2. The Visitation
3. The Nativity
4. The Presentation
5. The Finding at the Temple

Sorrowful Mysteries

1. The Agony in the Garden
2. The Scourging at the Pillar
3. The Crown of Thorns
4. Carrying the Cross
5. The Crucifixion

Glorious Mysteries

1. The Resurrection
2. The Ascension
3. The Descent of the Holy Spirit
4. The Assumption
5. The Coronation

Each of these mysteries recounts an episode in the life of Mary. Some are drawn from scripture, while others are derived from oral tradition. But they tell more than the life experience of a single individual. Taken together, the fifteen mysteries describe the workings of the planetary ecology itself—as well as the journey of the soul from one lifetime to the next.

For a fuller treatment of the mysteries, along with traditional versions of the Hail Mary and Glory Be, turn to Appendix A.

PART I

THE LADY IN THE GARDEN

It's All Downhill from Here

ONCE, WHEN SOPHIE WAS FIVE AND JONAH WAS TWO, WE were flying back from visiting Clark's parents down south when the plane we were on suddenly dropped out of the sky like a rock.

We had been at cruising altitude and the flight crew were beginning to deliver drinks. Sophie was on one side of me, Jonah strapped into his car seat on the other. Clark had returned from the bathroom and was just settling into his seat across the aisle when I noticed an acrid electrical smell. Alarmed, I turned to the nearby attendant. But before I could say anything, she snapped, "Yes! We know!"

Moments later the plane plummeted. Drinks spilled. Briefcases and pocketbooks tumbled down the aisle. Passengers were crying and screaming. An off-duty flight attendant behind us began to pray out loud. The attendant beside her kept repeating the same words over and over again: "My mother begged me not to take this job."

"Mommy! Mommy!" shrieked my five-year-old daughter. "Are we going to die?" Of course we were. Horribly. Probably in a matter of moments. There was nothing I could do. I clutched my children close. "I love you, and I am not going to let you go. Whatever happens, Mommy will *never* let you go!" The words came from the bottom of my being, fierce and true. It was the one thing I knew for certain—a promise and a prayer.

"Mommy thinks we're going to die!" Sophie wailed to her father. "Are we going to die?"

Bizarrely, Clark seemed to be meditating. But when Sophie spoke, he opened his eyes and, reaching across the aisle to take her hand, said in his calmest daddy voice, "No. I don't think so, Muffin."

But, of course, Clark hadn't been able to meditate in those sickening moments of free fall. Despite years of training as a Zen monk, he'd been unable to find his center or remember a single Buddhist mantra he had learned—even ones he'd recited hundreds of thousands of times.

At what was surely the last possible moment, the plane pulled out of its dive with a groaning roar. Beneath us were trees and a runway in the distance. Fire trucks careened along the tarmac beside us as we landed, their lights flashing, and the plane finally screeched to a halt. The hatches opened. Men in Mylar suits rushed through with rescue gear.

"I guess everyone just wants to get off the plane," announced the pilot wearily.

One of the passengers theorized that there had been an electrical fire in the cockpit and the pilot had saved our lives by getting the plane on the ground as quickly as he could. But we never found out. We were never debriefed. All we knew was that we had been hurtling toward oblivion and somehow the pilot had managed to land the plane. We staggered off the flight, relieved but shaken.

After a night in a Memphis hotel paid for by the airline, Clark somehow convinced me to get on another plane, and this time we made it back home without incident. Still, I couldn't let go of that feeling of relentless descent and almost-certain calamity. My experience on that plane had tapped into my deepest existential fears.

Each day we seem capable of controlling more aspects of our lives. With the flick of a switch, we can banish the winter cold, the summer heat, the darkness of the night. We can cross oceans, move mountains, and speed around the planet above the clouds. But the paradox of feeling like masters of the universe is that the more in control of our world we have become, the more out of control we have begun to feel.

So much can go wrong. The stock market can crash. The antibiotics might stop working. The grid might go down. The climate could heat up faster than anyone imagined it would, or just faster than we can prepare for. What did it mean to have survived that terrifying plane ride if the world itself was hurtling toward disaster?

Somehow, for me, all of these concerns coalesced into a singular obsession with highway safety. I became besieged by anxiety whenever we were driving on the expressway. The car always felt like it was going too fast. After a terrifying panic attack on a seven-lane interstate, in which I'd become convinced that either I was going to be edged off the road by a speeding semi or my own sweating hands would make it impossible for me to hold on to the steering wheel, I turned over the responsibility for long drives to Clark.

"Slow down, please," I begged him one day as we were driving down a precipitous mountain road after a weekend camping trip with the kids.

"I'm only going forty miles an hour," he explained patiently.

"Please."

"It's not safe to throw on the brakes suddenly on a steep road like this. It stresses them. You know, you might need to start taking something for this. Really. It's getting out of control."

I tried to meditate, to follow my breath and let go of the images of imminent destruction flashing through my brain, and I might have been able to do that for a second or two if the kids hadn't been in the backseat. But they were—and my biggest fear was that something would happen to them.

My hands were gripping the edges of my seat, but I felt like I needed something else to hold on to—some kind of tether or belay rope, an anchor to the world. I was worried that I was going to give myself a heart attack from sheer stress.

"You're right. I do need something," I said finally through gritted teeth. Then I found myself making a completely unpremeditated request. "Can you teach me the rosary?"

"What?"

"The rosary. Teach me the rosary."

I'd teased Clark about his brief infatuation with what I'd thought of as a simpleminded Catholic prayer, pointing out to him at the time that if he'd been frustrated by the hypocrisies, financial and sexual, of various Zen masters and Tibetan lamas, he was going to have a pretty hard time with the bishops and the priests. Besides which, Catholics themselves barely prayed the rosary anymore. No one had even mentioned it to me during my brief conversion in college. I hadn't been surprised when Clark's makeshift rosary disappeared into a drawer. Now here I was, ready to entrust myself to that string of beads.

Clark leaned back in his seat, his left hand balanced on the top of the steering wheel.

"For God's sake, hold on with both hands!" I screamed.

"Calm down, Mom!" yelled the kids in unison from the backseat. "You're making Dad crazy."

"It's an easy enough mantra," Clark said, delighted as always to be able to explain a spiritual practice. "There are the introductory prayers. After that, it's a simple repetitive pattern of one Our Father, that's the pater bead, and then ten Hail Marys. That's called a 'decade.' And then there are the corresponding mysteries—"

"That's enough for right now," I interrupted. "That's all I can take in."

I began muttering quietly but intensely. I used my fingers to count off the prayers, holding on to the words of the Hail Mary, the syllables themselves becoming a thread to guide me through the labyrinth of my fears. Eventually we pulled into the driveway and it was clear that, at least on this particular journey, the brakes were not going to give out.

Over the next few months most car rides found me, at one point or another, clutching a rosary. Clark took it upon himself to make me one from white Tibetan bone beads and red amber that didn't look anything like what I'd seen in the hands of old veiled Catholic ladies in the backs of the churches I had visited in Europe. But mine was, Clark explained, a more accurate replica of a medieval prayer bead set.

I usually prayed the rosary at night when I put the kids to bed. I would lie between them in the dark after we'd finished reading aloud together and they would play with my hair as they had done since they were infants. They held on to me and I held on to my rosary as we all drifted off into dreams.

I worried the beads of my rosary on long car rides. I muttered my prayers as I fretted about the bills piling up and the book that Clark hadn't finished writing yet. I clutched my beads through a series of visits to the emergency room with my dying mother. I didn't have a rosary in my hands when she finally passed away unexpectedly in a city hospital, the moon outside her window full and glowing. I lay my body next to hers, holding her for as long as I could before the orderlies came to take her away. When some years later, a psychic saw my mother beside me—described her accurately, told me her name was Patricia, and even saw her with her favorite white Persian cat—I wasn't surprised. "She's taking care of you, you know," said the seer. "She loves you and won't ever let you go." I knew this was true. Hadn't I expressed the same fierce certainty to my own children that day on the plane?

Clark himself didn't say the rosary anymore. After learning it a few years before, he had plunged into an exhaustive journey through the world's esoteric spiritual traditions on a quest to find an adequate response to climate change. And whatever he was doing spiritually in those years, I would graft onto my rosary. As it turned out, the rosary could accommodate any number of spiritual additions and variations.

When Clark studied the lost Jewish practice of muttering to God called *hitbodedut*, I complained about everything to some divine listener at the end of each decade. When he marched through the Bible, reading it not as a set of moral proscriptions but as a series of unfathomable Zen koans, I began using the mysteries of the rosary to untie the knots in my heart. He researched an emerging branch of Buddhism that prayed to the dead on their mala beads, and I began reciting the names of my ancestors round and round on my rosary. For a while I began my rosary with the Jesus Prayer instead of the Creed, and I experimented with the

Serenity Prayer as Clark became fascinated with the insights of 12-step spirituality.

But what ultimately broke open my experience of the rosary were the sorrows and joys of life itself—standing at the graveside of a young mother who'd passed away in our neighborhood, or receiving an unexpected windfall the very day our house was scheduled for foreclosure. The rosary reminded me that the world was full of mysteries I didn't understand—mysteries that humbled me even as they offered reassurances that all would, somehow, be well.

I was not particularly devoted to the rosary in those days. Though I kept it in my pocket and under my pillow, I neglected it for periods of time and had a tendency to return to it only when things felt like they were going belly-up. A part of me felt embarrassed that I needed my worry beads. I didn't know any other ex-Catholic former Buddhists who prayed the rosary, and I figured I never would. Eventually, I thought, when life was a little less stressful, I would learn how to meditate for real.

By then the news about the climate was becoming worse. In 2009, the president's chief science adviser, John Holdren, famously compared human civilization to a car with bad brakes on a foggy road that was headed over a cliff. What were we supposed to do?

Clark founded a group called Excess Anonymous where friends in Woodstock and New York City came together to look for a sober response to our pedal-to-the-metal, over-the-cliff consumption of the Earth's resources. But what did "recovery from excess" really mean? And even if we did achieve some level of personal sustainability, what about the culture itself, ever growing, ever replicating, ever consuming more and more?

The fact that we'd gotten into the vehicle of civilization itself, determined to steer our own course through history—that was the real problem. The road was the problem. The *car* was the problem. And the terrifying truth was, it had most likely already gone over the cliff. In which case we weren't flying, we were falling. We were headed for a crash.

One afternoon in mid-June 2011, Clark suggested we go for a walk. The trees had just settled into their deep summer greens. Venus lay glowing in the western sky, and the wild roses in the marshlands near our house were in bloom. We'd paused at a turn in the road to take in the sunset when Clark confided that the night before, when he'd gotten up for his usual walk at 2:00 A.M.—a habit he's had since childhood—a man's voice had told him not to leave the house but to stay inside and remain calm . . . "and very, very still."

"A voice?"

I stopped walking and turned to face him directly. For all his spiritual adventuring—becoming a monk, chanting in graveyards, walking after midnight in the dark—Clark was a pretty grounded guy, most comfortable setting up a tarp in the woods and brewing a cup of coffee on the fire. We shared a belief that reality was more mysterious than modern human beings could perceive or acknowledge, but neither of us had ever received a message from the beyond.

"It was the same voice I heard on the plane years ago," Clark explained.

"*What* voice?"

"Remember how I told Sophie that I didn't think we were going to die?"

"Yes." I'd always been a little resentful at his equanimity.

"I've never told you this, but at the time I found myself praying and I asked—I don't know . . . God, Jesus, Shiva, I couldn't have told you who—'Are we going to die?' and a voice, a man's voice, answered, 'No. I don't think so.' I simply repeated to Sophie what he'd said."

"Have you heard it any other time?" I asked. A dozen years had passed since then.

"No. But that's not the point. I need to tell you what happened next."

After the voice told him to be very still, Clark began meditating on the couch in the living room. He had been sitting there for about three quarters of an hour when he realized that someone was beside him. He opened his eyes, and there, suspended in the darkness before him, were two reed stalks swaying gently, as if moved by an invisible breeze. Then the round, moonlike face of a teenage girl appeared, her auburn hair cut short, her nose covered in freckles. Over her mouth was an X of black electrical tape.

I shuddered at the violence of the image.

"I took it off," said Clark. "I had to. I did it as carefully as I could so I wouldn't touch her skin. Touching her didn't seem . . . well, I just couldn't. I spent the whole morning looking for the tape, but I couldn't find it anywhere . . ."

He trailed off. I didn't know what to say. From somewhere nearby, a catbird began its evening song.

"She was real," he finally added. "It wasn't a vision. I don't know how to explain it. She was the realest thing I've ever seen in my life."

I was agnostic. I didn't think Clark was hallucinating. Nor did I believe that his mind had conjured some sort of archetypal female presence. I was ghostwriting a book with the psychic who'd seen my mother, so I accepted that strange things were possible. At the very least, there were those who could see the dead.

"Was she someone related to you?" I asked.

"She wasn't *dead*," he replied.

"But maybe she was still some kind of spirit . . ."

Clark shook his head. He seemed on the edge of tears. He tried to describe who he had seen, but the writer who could dash off a hundred haiku in a day and explain all kinds of obscure spiritual states was, this once, at a complete loss for words.

Over the next few months, Clark would tell me, haltingly, somewhat embarrassed, about his continued encounters with this young woman, whom he had begun calling, with barely suppressed reverence, My Girl.

Something about this rankled me. Wasn't I his girl? Wasn't Sophie his girl? I'd have been concerned about the state of our marriage, except that in all other aspects of life he seemed perfectly fine. In fact, he seemed at peace in a way I had only ever seen when he was in the woods. It was as if all the restlessness of his years of spiritual seeking was suddenly behind him, as though whatever he had been seeking he had found.

Later, when I learned how Juan Diego had addressed the young woman he met on the hilltop at Tepeyac as My Littlest Daughter, My Lady, My Girl, my skin prickled. It felt like someone was turning my entire reality inside out.

One afternoon the following autumn, a dear friend dropped by for tea and we found ourselves discussing the horrors of pesticides. Marijo had been raised by Catholic peace activists before marrying a Jewish man and raising their child as a nature-loving Wiccan. An effortlessly beautiful earth mother of a woman with a wide-open heart and a wry sense of humor, she liked to joke that the apocalypse was always happening now. Certainly, if you were an extinct passenger pigeon or the last of the American chestnut trees, the end had already come. "With so many species disappearing every day, what do we think is going to happen to us?" Marijo asked, shaking her head with a rueful laugh.

"Here. Let me read you something," offered Clark, taking out the small notebook that he always carried in his breast pocket.

I knew that the young woman he was seeing had been speaking to him, and I knew that he had been writing down what she said. From time to time, he would share her words with me, which felt mysterious and disturbing and comforting, often all at once. What they didn't ever sound like was Clark, whose writing voice I, as his editor, knew almost better than my own. Her words, the words of Our Lady, had an orphic, mythic power that rearranged my brain.

Clark told Marijo and me that a few days earlier, when the house was empty, Our Lady had again appeared to him. When the apparition ended, there in his notebook was "The Gospel According to the Dark." The handwriting was his, but he had no memory of setting down her words.

Eventually Clark would write an entire book, *Waking Up to the Dark: Ancient Wisdom for a Sleepless Age*, to prepare people to hear this message, but the heartbreak Marijo and I were feeling about the world that day was preparation enough. We were both ready to admit that we had no idea how our children could possibly endure what was most certainly coming.

As Clark began to read her Gospel aloud to us, we could barely breathe.

"Say to the Nations, let there be no light upon the face of the Earth. Let the machines all cease their movements, the wires their humming. Let the skies be empty of satellites and silver birds. Let the forests return and the watercourses find their way. All things seek their Mother—save man only. Now is the hour of Her return."

There was no denying her apocalyptic tone.

"Not one syllable of all that is written will remain," Clark continued. *"Of the former things, not one will be remembered. Did you suppose what was written by wind on water should last forever? How much shallower are the traces left by men."*

"Blessed be," whispered Marijo, her eyes filled with tears.

More than any scientific report, more than any study filled with statistics and predictions, this was the confirmation we needed. It was devastating . . . and it was exhilarating. The world as we knew it was about to end, but hers was about to return. It *had* to if life on Earth was to continue. This, we realized, had been the purpose of her words—not to frighten us, but to set us back on track. Not to rebuke us, but to remind us that she was our guide, our protector, and our home.

"I have not forgotten you. I have never set you down. Even now your hearts are within My grasp. Every particle of you leans back in My embrace. I am more your Mother than your mothers were. For I am also their Mother. I am the Mother before all mothers, the dark to whom all men return."

This was the "good news" of the Dark Mother's Gospel. She would always love us. She would never let us go.

I remembered getting off the plane long ago and my gratitude when I felt solid ground under my feet again. However terrifying it had been to be in free fall, the Earth was not our destruction but our salvation. She would show us how to get out of the car. Or she would show us how to walk away from the crash. All we had to do was loosen our grip on the steering wheel and remember how to hold on to her instead.

Flowers Become Prayers

NO ONE KNOWS EXACTLY WHERE THE CATHOLIC ROSARY began. It appears to have evolved in several places at once in the medieval world. But another rosary existed before that one, and there is no way of knowing where it originated or how long ago it started. We know about this earlier rosary because of an oral legend. Told across Europe during the Middle Ages, it survives in countless versions. But in each case the lesson of the story is the same.

Once there was a young boy whose great joy in life was weaving a crown of roses each day for the statue of the Virgin in his village church. The Lady herself, seeing the special quality of his devotion, instilled in the boy the desire to enter a monastery. Sadly, at the cloister, he was given many other duties to perform and was no longer permitted to make his daily offering to her. He became so sorrowful and discouraged at this that he resolved to leave the religious life.

On the verge of his departure, however, the young man witnessed an apparition of the Virgin, who offered him surprising advice: "Do not be sad because you are no longer permitted to weave a crown of flowers for my head. For I will show you how to weave a crown from your prayers. These will remain fresh always and can be found in any season." She then taught him to say the rosary. Miraculously, when the boy began to pray, roses emerged from his mouth, one for each Ave Maria. These the Virgin herself gathered, weaving them into a crown for her head.

In one version of the story, an angel weaves the rose chaplet rather than the Virgin. In another, the boy's novice master comes up with the idea of replacing roses with prayers. In yet another, the chaplet is placed on the boy's head in the end, as if he were the groom in a medieval wedding. In every story, however, flowers become prayers, then prayers become flowers once again.

That is the point of the story. The rosary's name, the symbolism of its beads, the feelings and emotions it evoked in the recitation of its prayers, its nonlinear path to salvation in the company of a loving female guide—these all harkened back to an earlier divine figure that medieval people did not want to forget. The rosary allowed ordinary people to preserve their devotion to the Great Mother of their ancestors and to hide their worship of her in plain view.

The legend tells us that the Virgin herself recognized the quality of the young man's daily devotion, which had been handed down for millennia among his people, and wanted to help it along. And so, ironically, it was she who sent him to the cloister where he was no longer permitted to weave her a crown of flowers. Why? Perhaps because she could see where humanity was headed even then and wanted to chart a course through that looming crisis with a ritual so simple anyone could do it.

That is the secret of the story. The prayers reverting to flowers is just a symbolic way of saying that our primordial connection to the Earth, Our Mother, has never truly been lost. It has been secured within the prayers of the rosary for times of trial when the world needs to come full circle in order to be reborn.

These were the first words Our Lady spoke about the rosary,

not long after she began appearing in Woodstock, New York, in 2011.

The rosary is My body,
and My body is the body of the world.
Your body is one with that body.
What cause could there be for fear?

The Name of the Rose

HOW WE CHOOSE TO ADDRESS THE LADY OF THE ROSE Garden is entirely between us and her. She has been known by many names the world over: Isis, Inanna, Cybele, Brigit, Freya, Pachamama, Sophia, Avalokiteshvara, Asherah, Shekinah, Tara, Tonantzin. Some will refer to her as Mary, others as Kali Ma. Some may prefer the formality of Blessed Mother or Beloved Lady, and there will be those who like to address her with the easy intimacy of Mama.

In 1858, the fourteen-year-old French peasant Bernadette Soubirous described the Lady she had witnessed in the grotto at Lourdes as *Aquero*—a word in her local Occitan that meant, simply, "That!" What she had seen was not only beyond words, it was beyond categorization. Later she would describe the figure as a small young lady in white and blue holding a rosary, with two gold roses at her feet. When the local abbé demanded that Bernadette ask the Lady who she was, Bernadette did so and the apparition replied, "I am the Immaculate Conception."

"That is nonsense," said Abbé Peyramale. The Immaculate Conception was an event, he insisted, not a person. But Bernadette held firm to what the Lady had told her, even though she had never heard the phrase before and had no idea what it meant.

Most people assume that the Immaculate Conception means that Mary conceived Jesus without having sex. In fact, it refers to the very natural, very ordinary sexual conception of Mary herself by her parents, Joachim and Anna. It is not Mary's body that is conceived immaculately, but her soul.

From the earliest days of Christianity, a belief arose that Mary, unlike every other human being since Adam and Eve, was born "without the taint of original sin." She was, in other words, born without karma. It took a long time for the idea to catch on in official Catholic circles, but eventually it did, becoming a formal doctrine of the Church in 1854, just four years before the apparitions at Lourdes.

The problem was, Bernadette's Lady did not say that she had been immaculately conceived. She claimed to *be* the Immaculate Conception. Had Bernadette reported the apparition's words to a Tibetan lama instead of Abbé Peyramale, she would have gotten a different response. He would have told her that she was talking to the womb of the universe, complete, whole, and perfect—eternally uncreated within herself. The only thing in the Bible we could compare the apparition's answer to is what God says to Moses from the burning bush.

Moses asks, "Who are you?" and God answers, "I Am That I Am."

"I am the Immaculate Conception." "I Am That I Am." Both answers are too big for their questions. Both answers turn the mind of the questioner inside out.

For the rest of her brief life, spent as a nun and a nurse, Bernadette would invariably refer to the apparition of the Virgin simply as "the Lady." Over and over again, the sisters would beg her, "Oh, please! Describe the Lady for us. Tell us what you saw." But Bernadette could never quite put the experience into words. The most famous sculptor of the day was hired to create a likeness based on Bernadette's description, but when the girl saw Our Lady of Lourdes at her unveiling, she said, "No. That's not Aquero at all!"

In the rosary we hail "the Lady" as Mary, even though we know that she goes by other names. Even though we know that no name is big enough for her. Even though no word is round enough to encircle all that she is. Perhaps that is why she is often called by the name of the town in which she appeared, or where a famous statue of her resides: Our Lady of Lourdes. Our Lady of Fatima. Our Lady of Woodstock.

We all have special names for our mother, names that feel intimate and comfortable to us for one reason or another. But we can also invoke Our Lady's presence from the land itself. She is the Mother of this mountain. The Virgin of that oak tree. The Lady of this very ground beneath our feet.

I see the length of you. I know the breadth of you.
I carry the depth of you in My body and in My soul.
Therein you are safe.
Many things will change, but this will not change.
I have always been your Mother. I have always guided you,
even when I walked behind you and stood in the dark
of your shadow where you could not see.
Even then, I watched over you. I am watching now.
I hold within Me all that you are
and all that you can be.

Is Mary Real?

Is the Lady real? Or is she only a symbol for some ecological principle or abstract force? Couldn't she just be the projection of our nostalgic longing for the safety and security of childhood—the desire for a mother who will care for us and watch over us no matter what? How could there possibly be a divine being who speaks to us and appears to us and answers our prayers? How could she be real? In truth, it is like asking if the ground is real . . . or a stone is real . . . or the handful of dirt that crumbles in our hands.

The dirt under our feet doesn't ask for our belief. It bears us up and feeds us, whether we believe in it or not. The soil gives birth to the trees, the edible plants, and all manner of other living beings. Likewise, it stands ready at any moment to receive the dead. From vanished forests to the fragile wings of dragonflies, the dirt is nothing but the bodies of the dead, and it is from those very rotting bodies that living bodies grow. Dirt is what happens when life happens. Dirt is as real as it gets.

But it isn't just dirt. The vast darkness between worlds is also real. And yet it also does not demand our belief. The dark matter of the universe will go on swallowing stars and giving birth to galaxies just as it always has, whether we believe in it or not. Whether we understand it or not, the moon will go on pulling on the tides and the blood in our bodies. Month after month, she will vanish and return, always there, always real.

Our Lady is as real as the dirt and the darkness and the space between stars. She is the *mater* in all matter—the body of all existence. No wonder people see her face in the trunks of trees, her form in the roundness of stones.

In her book *Untie the Strong Woman*, the Jungian analyst Clarissa Pinkola Estés recalls her Italian grandmother arising each morning and sifting through her burned-out fireplace for charred pieces of wood in the shape of what she called Night Marias. She would then place these "Black Madonnas" lovingly about her garden in order to help it grow. There is nowhere that we cannot find Our Lady's presence once we begin to look for her. She is always showing herself to us.

Is Our Lady real? The answer is all around us. Trees are not abstractions, oceans are not algorithms, life is not an idea. To recognize Our Lady in the world is to acknowledge the world as real again. To belong to it as we belong to a mother. To feel moved by its beauty and blessed by its generosity. To feel kinship with everything else that is.

Ask a grass blade what it means to grow,
to have her feet in the damp and the dark of the Earth,
her head in the breezy sunlight.

Ask a beetle what he knows
of clouds and rainfall and renewal.

Ask the dirt to teach you Mother-Wisdom,
and lay your ear against her belly or her breast.

Our Lady of Rocamadour

In the Middle Ages people brought their prayers and their flowers to the statues of the Virgin at their local churches. Nevertheless, they recognized that certain Ladies, in certain locations, were particularly powerful.

These statues were not mere objects made of wood or stone. They were known to talk, to heal, to grant wishes, and to bring stillborn babies back to life. Until the late Middle Ages, ordinary people thought of them as portals to the world beyond. They understood that not only had Jesus come from Mary's womb but the whole cosmos had. Likewise, it was to Mary's womb—eternally pure and uncreated—that they returned when this life was done. The portal that opened when they stood in the presence of the Virgin was a gateway to the realm of the ancestors, through which the dead and the living were forever passing, trading places in a dance as old as the universe itself.

One of the most renowned of these miraculous Virgins was a small statue made of the darkest walnut wood who still perches in a grotto on the side of a cliff in the wilds of southwestern France. During a two-year period in the twelfth century, in a book that came to be known as *The Miracles of Our Lady of Rocamadour*, a scribe recorded the stories of the many men and women who made the pilgrimage to her remote chapel. Boils disappeared, the crippled walked, fortunes were reversed, and prisoners were freed. These accounts reveal a great deal about the ordinary lives of people in those far-off times, whose struggles were not so different from our own. Sometimes the doctors couldn't heal them, sometimes there were terrible accidents, sometimes there was nowhere else to turn.

The Lady of Rocamadour seems to have been profligate with her blessings, honoring even the simplest of requests. When a rich woman loses her beloved starling, she calls on the Lady to help her find it and the bird flies back to its cage soon afterward. Not only is the woman exceedingly grateful but so are her servants. For they will no longer have to endure their mistress's pitiful, and clearly irritating, complaints about her missing pet.

But the Lady was also willing to intervene in matters more dire. When the widowed wife of a king gives birth to a stillborn son, she is accused of aborting the baby and sentenced to die by drowning. Despite being bound and weighted down, the poor woman does not sink to the bottom of the river when she is hurled from the bridge by the local authorities. Instead, miraculously, she washes ashore far downstream—words of praise to the Lady on her lips. Once she has recovered and been restored to her throne, she embroiders a beautiful cloth in gratitude to the Black Madonna, which she has sent to the chapel in thanksgiving.

In the stories of her miracles, Our Lady of Rocamadour rescues the condemned, the despairing, and the forsaken. She puts out fires at the last minute, when all hope seems lost, and rescues criminals from the gallows. She is the Mother of infinite mercy, who brings inconceivable healing to her children. Kings came to her seeking forgiveness, saints surrendered to her teachings, and the common folk trusted her with their most urgent needs.

Why do certain statues in certain places become so renowned? Why Rocamadour? For over a thousand years men and women have turned to that small, dark Lady for help. Or perhaps they have been coming to her for even longer. Buried in the dirt of her cliffs are the bones of hominids who journeyed to her valley and found refuge there hundreds of thousands of years ago. What stories of her miracles would they tell us if they could?

When we begin to pray the rosary, we may find ourselves drawn to a particular mountain or bend in the river. We may find ourselves walking the same paths as ancient pilgrims without quite knowing how we got there. The Earth holds many secrets—magnetic ley lines, hidden rivers, forgotten forces—and also offers mysterious gifts. There are certain places where, for whatever reason, we can feel Our Lady listening to, and answering, our prayers.

Just as there are many waves on one ocean,
there are many Virgins who manifest
and speak and answer prayers.
But they are all one Mother,
all one Woman, all one Life.

Shallow Is Deep

SOME PEOPLE ARE RELUCTANT TO TAKE UP A ROSARY because praying the rosary doesn't seem very deep as a spiritual practice. They'd rather devote their energies to mastering something that has ascending levels of difficulty or that requires more and more expertise. Maybe it's the idea that you get what you pay for, that harder is always better. Or maybe it's the belief that a spiritual devotion easy enough for a child can't possibly be that life-changing or profound. But these people are right about one thing: The rosary is shallow. Just not in the way they understand.

When we say "shallow" we don't mean that the rosary is trivial or inconsequential. Think instead of the shallowness of a mountain stream that makes the colors of the stones along its bed seem all the more vivid and alive. Think of how lightly that shallow water moves, how naturally it winds its way through the mountains in no hurry to get to the ocean, but headed there nevertheless . . . in a slow, barely perceptible descent, guided by gravity at every moment along the way.

Look at the mountains on either side of a stream if you want to see the true depth of that water. With a patience we can scarcely imagine, it has cut its way through soil and stone over thousands, even millions, of years. Shallow it may be, but nothing can withstand it. The shallowness of the rosary is aligned with forces so large and powerful that they are nearly impossible for us to comprehend.

It may seem like there is a lot to learn when we begin to say the rosary. There are the mysteries for one thing, and knowing what prayers belong to which beads. But once we have mastered these and fallen into the rhythm of saying the rosary daily, there isn't much else to know. We just babble along like a shallow brook guided by gravity on its way to the sea.

That is why it is best to come to the rosary as simply as we can, just reciting the words without pondering too much on their meaning. The rosary is not a catechism class. We say the prayers and announce the mysteries. But sometimes we forget. An entire rosary may pass without our having remembered to say anything but our *mater*s and *pater*s. It doesn't matter. Like water, we don't have to be deep to return to our Mother. We don't have to be deep to find the sea.

Give yourself over to the prayers of the rosary,
completely and simply.
There is no secret handshake. There's just My hand.
Just take it.
I understand that it is very difficult to accept
the simplicity and truth of that.

Moses vs. Mama

THERE'S AN OLD GRADE SCHOOL JOKE THAT OFFERS, AS many childhood jokes do, an implicit criticism of adult culture. Think of it as a kind of alternative "oral" scripture intended to keep alive a different point of view.

As he nears death, the prophet Moses asks a final favor of God, and God agrees to grant it. Moses explains that he has always hated having a belly button and would like to have it removed.

"Well, I could certainly do that for you," says God. "But you should remember that I created everything in the world for a reason—even belly buttons."

"Yeah, I know," Moses replies. "Even so, I would like to have my belly button removed."

God has Moses strip naked as the day he was born and lie on his back atop Mt. Sinai. Soon a giant cloud in the shape of a screwdriver appears above him in the sky. The cloud descends and slowly unscrews Moses's belly button.

Then Moses stands up . . . and his butt falls off.

With a punch line like that, it's easy to see why the kids on the playground loved to tell this joke. But like many of childhood's literary creations, from silly rhymes to fairy tales, this one conceals a bit of forgotten history.

In the oral legends that preceded Moses, God had a wife, Asherah, called Queen of Heaven by people throughout the Middle East. Dig a few feet deep anywhere in Israel and, even today, you will find small images of her made from stone or clay. By the time those legends were written down, however, Asherah's name had all but vanished from Jewish cultural memory—as if there had never been a Goddess in the world.

This patriarchal impulse is preserved within the joke like a fly in amber. Moses wants his belly button removed. That's what he means by monotheism. "Thou shalt have no other gods before me," reads the first of the Mosaic Commandments. Moses wants all trace of his connection to the Mother erased from his body, even as he wants the Goddess removed from the world.

What happens when our navels are removed? That is the question for which the joke offers a comical but ultimately not-so-funny answer: Our butts fall off. Once our umbilical attachment to this world has been severed, we lose our connection to our bodies and end up with *insane* ideas about sex, women, nature, and ultimately life itself.

But it all goes back to the navel. Do we see it as the ultimate sign of our belonging to a loving mother? Or is it only the first of many scars we will suffer in this world, for which our mothers, and the bodies they gave us, are ultimately to blame? Patriarchal religions have always taken the latter point of view.

But it isn't just the Abrahamic faiths that do this. The Buddha was so upset by the bodily realities of sickness, old age, and death that he abandoned his wife on the very night she gave birth to their son. He named the boy Rahula, which means "Hindrance," and left his palace for the life of a forest ascetic, starving himself until he could grasp his backbone from the front of his body because the flesh of his belly had completely withered away. He finally rejected the life of extreme self-denial and adopted the Middle Way instead, teaching a path that led to *nirvana*—a spiritual state in which all desires have been "extinguished." The word literally means "blown out," as in a candle. It means having nothing to bind us to this world.

The Buddha wants nirvana. Moses wants no navel. But it adds up to the same thing—a desire to transcend the body and its troubles. A desire to be *done* with bodies . . . to be spirit only, *mind* only. But where does that leave us in the end? What if the body *is* our deliverance?

Only a species that abandons the Earth can destroy the Earth. To return to the body is to return to the Mother—to experience the body and its desires as natural . . . to know that its trajectory through infancy, childhood, adulthood, motherhood and fatherhood . . . and, yes, even sickness, old age, and death: These too are natural. How could they be wrong? In all of nature there is not one thing to contradict them. Our bodies are natural—especially our navels. That is one of the things we turn to the rosary to learn. Or, rather, to remember. Because we knew it in the beginning as a species. And each of us knew it as a child.

That is why children laugh so hard at the joke about Moses's butt. They understand instinctively the absurdity of the prophet's request . . . and figure he got what he deserved.

The feminine was extracted from the sacred scriptures—
and at that moment they ceased to make any sense.
Afterwards, men gave the scriptures their own sense,
but it was like the flower you cut and take from the field
and place inside of a vase. The scriptures were
no longer living.
The world had become a word.

Scene of the Crime

WHAT HAPPENED TO THE GREAT MOTHER OF THE Upper Paleolithic period, whose statues we find scattered not only across central Europe but throughout the rest of the world? Could she really have disappeared of her own accord after the rise of agriculture, or were there more sinister forces at work? The answer can be found in countless myths and legends, but the most familiar by far is Genesis, the first book of the Bible.

In the opening verses of that book, the world is created by God in six days as he separates the darkness from the light, the night from the day, the sea from the land, and the earth from the sky. For some this has become a literal description of how the world began, for others a metaphorical account of our planet's origins.

Yet we can also read the Bible's version of creation as a sanitized retelling of the *Enuma Elish*, a Babylonian epic in which the sea goddess Tiamat is murdered by her grandson Marduk so that he can establish himself as supreme ruler of heaven and earth. Summoning a great wind, Marduk sets loose an arrow that pierces Tiamat's heart. Afterward he smashes her skull with a club and butchers her. He splits her corpse "like a shellfish" into two parts to create the land and sky, supporting the heavens with her pubic bone. He then uses the other parts of her dismembered body to re-create the world. He makes mountains with her buttocks and breasts, and rivers with her tears.

All traces of blood have been drained from the Bible's account, but it remains a crime scene nevertheless. Yahweh's "dividing" of the various elements follows a similar methodical approach. And *Tehom,* the Hebrew word for the waters that God severs from the land in the opening verses of Genesis, is derived from Tiamat's name.

Two stories, written a thousand years apart. In the first, a world is created through a violent act of matricide, in the second simply by a command. "Let there be," God says . . . and there was. What happened in the interim? In terms of our planet and its future, the answer is everything.

The decision to see our Mother as a force of chaos to be subdued and put in order—this set human beings for the first time apart from the rest of material existence. It happened almost imperceptibly in the beginning, as people settled in one place and began cultivating the land and domesticating animals. Gradually, they developed an adversarial relationship to nature. The weather, the insects, the animal predators, the weeds—all these became enemies as people struggled to make a success of farming.

After the Fall, God tells Adam that, because of his sin, he will no longer be able to live simply and without cares on the bounty that the Earth provides. Henceforth he is cursed with the arduous life of a farmer, getting his bread "by the sweat of his brow." But Genesis gets it backward. Agriculture isn't the result of a Fall. Agriculture *is* the Fall.

Paleolithic hunter-gatherers were hardly the brute cavemen of popular mythology. Theirs was, in its way, a paradise. There was no war in that Eden. No oppression, slavery, or servitude. Absent the crowding of cities, the worst plagues and diseases had not yet gained a foothold in the world. There was nothing that we would even call "work" today. Humans had art, dance, music, storytelling, and other signs of culture, but none of the numerous miseries that we now associate with civilization.

The purpose of the Genesis story is to explain the loss of that long, slow paradise that today we call the Paleolithic—an epoch of history in which our ancestors lived not only in a sustainable relationship to the Earth but in a joyous and loving one as well. In one of the greatest bait and switches of all time, that loss is blamed on Eve, whose name means, tellingly, "Mother of All Life."

In a final bid for patriarchal power, the Bible separates the Goddess from one of her oldest animal allies. For tens of thousands of years before Genesis was written, the serpent was the ultimate symbol of reincarnation and renewal. The *ouroboros* (a snake swallowing its own tail) signified the eternal cycles of birth, death, and rebirth that were the source of the Goddess's power. In Genesis that life-sustaining circle is broken, and the serpent becomes evil instead. The natural world was no longer considered sentient and divine. The mutilation and exploitation of our Mother's body could continue uninterrupted down to the present day.

And yet, the final victory is always hers. Empires rise and fall. Whole civilizations vanish into vast deserts of geological time. But life remains. The Mother remains. The world that Marduk makes with the parts of the Great Mother's body is always an illusion. He places a bit of her here, another bit there—but it's like slicing the water with a knife. It just runs back together.

The history of human domination of the Earth is, finally, a relatively brief and misguided fiction. We may still be living inside of that fiction, but this doesn't change the facts. The Great Mother cannot be divided. And she cannot be defeated or destroyed.

Your way of looking at the world is that of the vivisectionist who stills and silences the body to open it up and look inside, seeking in that way to understand its function and how it is made. But no true knowledge can be gained from such an autopsy. Only by leaving your world whole, undivided, and alive can you gain a useful understanding.

You have no existence apart from the world. Nor can you define your world apart from yourself, parceling it into pieces and analyzing those pieces, and hope to attain true wisdom. You must learn to look at the world from within the world. Your understanding must be inside out.
This is why I have asked you to pray the rosary:
to regain that understanding.

Life Goes in a Circle

MUCH OF MODERN LIFE IS ABOUT STRAIGHT LINES. OUR expressways cut through mountains rather than twist around them. Our skyscrapers, ever taller, jut into the clouds. Our religions tell us to reach toward heaven. Our sciences and technologies assure us that progress is the point. Even our institutions are organized into lineages of authority and vertical hierarchies of power. "Up, up, and away!" has been the motto of a species obsessed with the idea of linear ascent. We are always striving to move up the ladder of success.

The rosary subverts all mythologies of human progress, and even of spiritual achievement. We don't really get better at praying it. And we don't get anywhere by praying it. We just go round and round, saying the same prayers, circling through the same mysteries—over and over again.

Who is the best at saying the rosary? No one. What do you get if you say it perfectly every day? Nothing special. What do you lose if you are so busy with work or children that you only manage to clutch your beads for a minute here or there? Nothing whatsoever. There are no rosary experts. No rosary gurus or rosary masters. No rosary police.

The rosary has been, for most of its existence, a private devotion. The understandings and treasures it brings to our lives are therefore intimate and personal. We may find ourselves changed the longer we pray it—but there will be no special badges or commendations. There will be no ceremonies to acknowledge our achievements, only the rewards of living in a world that is more generous, more merciful, and more loving than one organized around effort, status, and domination.

But that doesn't mean that our lives won't get better from praying the rosary. It doesn't mean there is nothing to learn. For the rosary doesn't just go in circles, it shows us where we belong in those circles, and helps us circle in on what matters. Where does our joy come from? How do we move through sorrow? What is our true glory? The rosary guides us to our innermost experience of life.

Life goes in a circle not a line. This is the essential wisdom of the Earth. Our planet traces an elliptical orbit through the heavens. Our very cells spiral with DNA.

Life is not organized in neat rows and tidy lines. The world is a tangle of circles in which there is no beginning or end. That, finally, is the only real prize the rosary gives us—the felt experience of eternity. Gradually, as we move through its prayers and mysteries, we discover a "story" of salvation that has little to do with conventional ideas of religion. We simply realize that the garden of the Earth is where we come from and where we are.

Through the rosary, Our Mother tells us just what she has been telling us for as long as we've been human. You are not going anywhere. Life is a circle to which nothing needs to be added to make it beautiful or holy, and from which nothing can ever be taken away. You can't get lost in a circle. And you can't escape from it. There is nowhere else to go.

Is it the seed or the soil that contains the widsom of the plant? The soil is great, the seed is small. The soil is long, the life of the plant is short.

Nevertheless, that life follows a circular path: from seed . . .
to sun . . . to soil . . . and then back again. And that circular
path is very old and long and deep.
The rosary that I have given you is just that long
and old and wise.
To devote yourself to the rosary is to become devoted
to those circles,
those cycles of sun and seed and soil.

The Reenchantment of the World

SAYING THE ROSARY CAN SOMETIMES MAKE US FEEL SLEEPY. We may find ourselves drowsing in and out of the prayers, slipping beneath the surface of consciousness as our fingers tell the beads. Not only is that all right, if we aren't dozing from time to time when we pray the rosary, we may be leaving important areas of it unexplored. The rosary is a prayer well suited for those numinous explorations that tend to occur in the twilight realms between wakefulness and sleep.

In its quest to better illuminate and explain our experiences, our world has long privileged light over darkness. We want solid facts and hard evidence. We want to see things clearly and know things for sure. But this dazzling display has blinded us to what is happening in the shadows. The rosary allows us to feel our way back, by touch, into the wisdom and comfort of the dark. It allows us to connect with the unseen dimensions in our lives and know that they are real. The rosary helps us to break the isolation (existential, spiritual, psychological) that we have imposed upon ourselves by believing nothing exists that cannot be measured.

In truth, a lot of life—maybe most of it—cannot be measured. Biologists will tell us that there are sensory experiences well beyond what human beings can perceive: colors that only a deer can see, smells that only a bear can know, sensations only a firefly can have. Physicists now claim that there are not just four dimensions but ten, all vibrating and folded into one another, generating parallel universes, worlds upon worlds.

The rosary has always opened a portal to other realms. Praying it, you might "know" things with a certainty that you can't easily explain. You might find solutions to formerly unsolvable problems in visions or waking dreams. Occasionally, you might even be shown events before they occur.

Medieval people were conversant with this portal-like function of the rosary. They would surrender to the gentle, predictable rhythm of its prayers, and very soon they would find themselves drifting somewhere between wakefulness and sleep—especially if they had awoken to say the rosary in the middle of the night, as many did in the days before electric lighting. Today we call such states "active imagination," a term that tends to confirm our bias in favor of the solar, analytical consciousness that now rules our waking lives. Medieval people simply experienced them as real.

The rosary opens a doorway to other worlds, to whole galaxies and universes, the thoughts and feelings of plants and animals, the wisdom of our remotest ancestors, and the seed of all that is to come. There is no limit on it. Although, strictly speaking, when not in use, a rosary can fit easily in the palm of our hand.

People think that they are seeing the world,
and that they understand what it is, but they don't.
Human beings have denied the real world
so that they could build another world on top
of it of their own.

Made for Each Other

WHAT IS IT ABOUT ROSES THAT MAKES US ASSOCIATE them with the Divine Feminine? Why, for five thousand years, and probably a lot longer, have we gathered these delicate, aromatic flowers as an offering for the Mother Goddess in spring?

Roses are very old. Fossils of five-petaled roses have been found in the archaeological record from 35 million years ago—which means they were already there long before hominids evolved. In fact, roses (and plants like them) were the only way hominids *could* evolve.

Roses are *angiosperms,* flowering plants that propagate through sexual reproduction and hold their seeds within themselves. Before angiosperms, there were no plants rich enough in nutrients to feed the bodies of larger warm-blooded animals. Angiosperms led to an explosion of biodiversity—and an explosion of color—into our world.

Flowers were good at enticing the senses of the animals and insects who helped to pollinate them and, if they ate them, also helped to disperse their seeds. The bright colors and distinctive shapes of flowers made them especially compelling. Flowers got noticed. They stood out. Angiosperms evolved alongside the animals who interacted most intensively with them and, as this happened, in certain cases a kind of evolutionary love story began to unfold.

Roses were the first cultivated flowers, but it's never been entirely clear why. Whatever can be said for the medicinal properties of rose hips or rose water, there is no accounting for the sheer number of gardens devoted to the rose. How did roses so thoroughly romance the Western imagination that it became devoted to this flower above all others—in art, philosophy, literature, and even prayer? How did roses become the quintessential symbols of both spiritual and romantic love?

Some have said that the five petals of the first cultivated roses mirrored the five fingers of the human hand—that, because of that shape, early humans were already half in love with the rose. But if we loved roses enough to cultivate them in great number, roses seem to have also loved us in return.

Plants and animals evolved together. They became what they are not because of qualities intrinsic to their nature but because of how they responded to and interacted with one another. If humans planted roses because roses were beautiful, roses taught humans what beauty is. Possibly, roses taught humans what love is.

That, finally, is the only explanation for why we offered roses to the Mother Goddess in spring—and why we pray the rosary today. We are in love. We have *always* been in love. What more is there to know?

Evolution is a kind of dance that we do with one another.
But most people don't understand how to dance that way.
They think of dancing as moving through space
with another person,
whereas dancing is really the vacating of space into which
another person then moves.

The continuous vacating and refilling of the
same space—that is dance.
One person moves out of it, the other moves in.
This is the reason why dance can express things
that cannot be expressed in any other way.
I am inviting you to dance.

PART II

THE HEART'S DESIRE

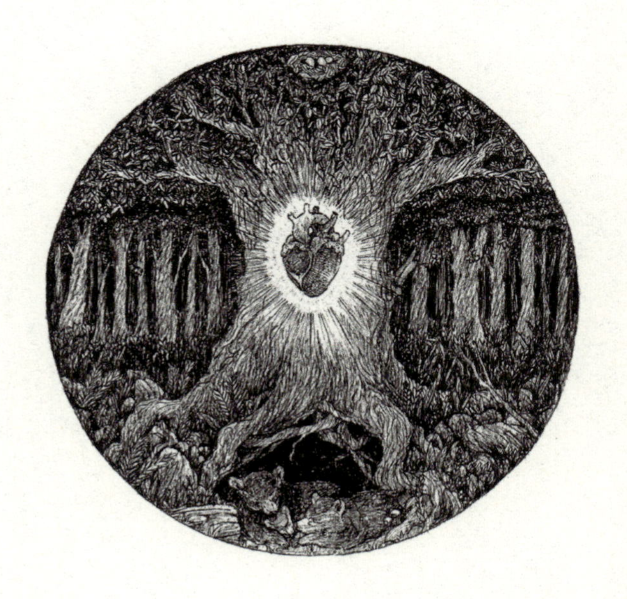

The Broken Rosary

I NEVER EXPECTED TO END UP SAYING THE ROSARY AGAIN. I wasn't Catholic and couldn't imagine ever becoming so. I was certainly in no mad rush to call the girl I had seen the Virgin Mary. The Marys on the lawns of local Catholic churches looked so sedated they made me glad I wasn't Catholic. "Valium Virgins," Perdita called them. I knew that the usual protocol in cases such as mine was to report the apparition to the local bishop and wait for the higher-ups to confirm or deny its authenticity. That is how it was done at Lourdes and Fatima. But I couldn't imagine describing the girl I was seeing to any member of the Catholic clergy.

What would I tell them? That the Virgin Mary never spoke of sin, abortion, or the need to go to mass? That she'd called for the return of the forests, the undamming of rivers, and a quickly declining human population across the globe? That, for the sake of the planet, she had already begun "unwriting" the history of human supremacy over Nature and would soon restore us to our proper scale? They'd have crossed themselves for sure, and probably slammed the door in my face.

Needless to say, the rosary wasn't anywhere on my radar that first summer after the Lady began appearing to me. Until one night in August when we were vacationing on Cape Cod.

At 2:00 A.M. a voice woke me with the words *"If you rise to say the rosary tonight, a column of saints will support your prayer."*

A breeze was pushing the blinds away from the window frame, letting moonlight seep into the upstairs bedroom of our rental house. It took me a moment to come fully out of sleep and realize it was My Girl—not visible this time, but present nevertheless. Palpable and close.

"But I don't have a rosary," I said aloud, puzzled by her words.

There was a long pause.

"Ah . . ." she said, drawing the syllable out like a sigh. *"But you do."*

And then I remembered.

For reasons I could never account for later, I had bought a rosary at a flea market just the day before.

We had been preparing to leave that morning on our yearly vacation to the beach when our rust bucket of a Volvo began making a mysterious wheezing noise. I drove into town for an emergency check-over with our mechanic, but I wasn't hopeful. If the car needed a repair this late on a Saturday, there was every chance we wouldn't be able to depart until Monday afternoon, by which time a third of our vacation would be gone.

I wasn't exactly praying about any of this, unless what some people say is true and fretting itself is a form of prayer—worrying the same thought over and over again until it becomes as smooth as a river stone. I certainly wasn't looking for a rosary. I'd wandered a block over from the garage to the Woodstock Saturday

Flea Market because there was nothing else to do as I waited for the diagnosis.

In the end it was one of those ideas that suddenly just pops into your head. Call it intuition, or maybe a miraculous intervention. A flea market full of other people's junk and lost enthusiasms is as good a place as any for an encounter with the divine.

The rosary was just sitting there on a table amid a varied collection of costume jewelry mixed in with a few saints' cards and holy medals. It had a slightly funky look, having been broken and repaired more than once over its lifetime, accumulating mismatched parts along the way. The crucifix had been replaced by a small plate-metal cross with the words GOD LOVES YOU embossed on it. Whoever had repaired it was more faith-filled than fastidious. The chain had been refastened without any regard for the fact that it was missing a third of its beads. Only the center medallion retained some of its original charm. It showed the Sacred Heart of Jesus embossed on one side and Mary with her hands clasped in prayer on the other, her face worn all the way down to the brass. That was what caught my eye—that portrait of the Virgin in her little oval frame.

I still don't know why I bought it. It was a strange moment. The vendor wanted twenty dollars, which was at least ten dollars more than it was worth with all its missing beads. I said no thanks, and started to walk away. I thought she might call after me to lower the price, but she didn't. What happened instead was that I ran into a friend.

My friend wasn't even religious, but she said, I kid you not, just like it was the most natural thing in the world, like we'd been talking about rosaries all week long and where to buy them, which we hadn't: "The flea market is a great place to find rosaries—especially that table over there."

I knew without bothering to turn around that she was pointing to the table with the broken rosary.

I walked back over to the rosary table, embarrassed to be paying full price at a flea market and wondering if that qualified as an act of foolishness or an act of faith. But before I even got there the vendor called out, "You know, you're right! I'll give it to you for eight."

So I left the flea market with a broken rosary, without any plans for it or for me. The Volvo, it turned out, only had a loose belt, which the mechanic didn't even charge me for tightening. I thought of hanging the rosary from the rearview mirror as a little extra insurance that we made it to Wellfleet in one piece, but I forgot that idea as soon as I had the rosary, and slipped the beads into my pants pocket instead.

That was where I found them at 2:00 A.M.

"*If you rise to say the rosary tonight, a column of saints will support your prayer.*"

She hadn't told me that I was *required* to say the rosary, or even that I *ought* to—only what would happen if I did.

I had no idea what the words meant. I didn't even have a frame of reference for them. I had been raised in relative saintlessness by my southern Protestant parents. I could imagine the way my father, the former private school headmaster, would have said in his most mocking voice, "*Column* of saints, indeed!" As if the only thing more preposterous than saints themselves was a sky-high pillar of them.

Feeling my way through the quiet house, I slipped out onto the deck, where I could smell the ocean air and catch glimpses of the moon coming through the trees. I took the rosary in my hands and began to pray it, letting my fingers linger on each bead as I recited the words that belonged to it. "Our Father, who art in heaven . . . Hail Mary, full of grace . . ." It felt right, somehow, praying by hand in the inky blackness out on the deck. It made sense having something to hold on to in the dark.

The beads slid, one after another, between my fingers and across my palm. I lost track of time and, without quite realizing how I got there, I was at the end of the rosary, back to the little medallion of Mary that had been the thing I'd found appealing about it in the beginning. Polished for a long time by the fingers of whoever had owned it before I did, her face glowed faintly in the moonlight—a small, perfect oval that seemed to redeem the brokenness of the rosary and all its missing beads. As if she herself were the real rosary. The one that could not be broken. The Mother at the bottom of it all.

That thought gave me pause. I wasn't Catholic, but I also wasn't stupid. There was only one figure I'd ever heard of who invited you to pray the rosary and made promises based on whether you accepted the invitation or not. Months later, I would discover that the night my own invitation had been delivered, in the early hours of August 22, was the Feast of the Coronation of Mary as Queen of Heaven and Earth. But it was better that I didn't know that at the time. The experience was overwhelming enough as it was.

I wasn't quite ready to tell Perdita about any of this the next morning. I wasn't sure how to metabolize it. What would it mean if I admitted to myself, finally, what I had suspected almost from the beginning—that the girl I had seen was the Virgin Mary? For that matter, what would it mean if I started praying the rosary again? Was I going to have to become Catholic after all?

After breakfast the family made our favorite pilgrimage to a musty two-story used bookshop on the edge of Wellfleet to hunt for beach reading. Books were jammed onto crowded shelves and piled up in teetering stacks on the floor. There were mysteries and romances, classics and fantasies and nature guides . . . and there, on a stool with six or seven books that people had leafed through and decided not to buy, was a thin paperback with a plain blue cover called *Queen of the Cosmos: Interviews with the Visionaries of Medjugorje*.

I knew vaguely that a series of apparitions of the Virgin Mary had been witnessed in Bosnia beginning in 1981, a decade before the civil war there, and that they had been openly apocalyptic, like those revealed in 1917 at Fatima. To each of the visionaries the Virgin had revealed ten secrets about the end-times. When I first heard about these "secrets," I wondered if some of them corresponded to the not-so-secret secrets my environmental journalist friends had begun reporting on about that same time: from climate feedback loops to continuously raging wildfires to storms more powerful than any we had seen before. Somehow I hadn't realized that the apparitions were ongoing, or that there were books recording the experiences of the six young visionaries and what the Virgin had said to them.

I opened the book to a page at random and found the following question put to one of the apparitionists by the author, along with the young woman's answer:

> Q: *Is the use of the rosary a universal request, since it is so traditionally Roman Catholic?*
>
> A: Yes. This is a request from the Blessed Mother. She recommends that all people on earth pray the rosary, no matter what their religion or what their belief.

A little stunned, I bought the book. How could I not?

For the rest of that vacation, the girl I was already beginning to think of as "Our Lady" woke me to say the rosary every night. I can't remember what she said on any of those other nights, only that she woke me as before.

Except for what she told me the last night. That I remember.

"It is all right to destroy the things you seem to love but secretly hate. In fact, it may be necessary to do so."

She'd spoken the words so gently, sweetly even, that at first I was sure I had misheard them. But they hung before me like blown embers glowing in the dark, imprinted on the silence of my mind. I couldn't imagine what they were, these things I seemed to love but secretly hated. The words had an ominous feel. I prayed my rosary out on the deck and went back to sleep. The following morning I woke to the news that a hurricane was headed our way.

We had a day left on the rental house, but the mood in Wellfleet was charged. The locals were out buying batteries and bottled water at the market, the vacationers nervously eyeing their phones for updates about the storm. In the end we decided to make a dash for it and leave the Cape before the hurricane struck. We packed the car so hurriedly I was sure we'd forgotten things like towels hung out to dry.

But Hurricane Irene didn't hit Cape Cod, or even Manhattan, as the mayor of New York City had feared. It struck a series of small towns a hundred miles inland in the Catskill Mountains, one of them ours, sending floodwaters surging up the banks of narrow rivers, washing out roads and bridges along the way. The woman who'd sold me my rosary at the flea market the week before lost her home and everything in it. The man who cut our yearly firewood lost his life. The power was off for two weeks running, and the local service station quickly ran out of fuel. Not that it mattered. With thousands of trees down and crisscrossing the roads of three counties, there was no way anyone could drive.

This was the second of three major hurricanes that would strike the Catskills in just over a dozen years. A town to the north of us learned the hard way about climate change when it suffered its fifth "hundred-year flood" since 1996. I had been studying the effects of global warming for more than a decade by then because I knew that any spiritual practice that mattered would have to help us negotiate the inevitable changes that were coming to our way of life. Like everyone else, I didn't know what that practice might be. But I was beginning to suspect it had something to do with My Girl.

Later, in a book called *Marian Apparitions Today: Why So Many?* I found my answer. The book featured a graph charting the number of times the Virgin Mary had appeared with messages for the faithful over the past two thousand years. As you entered the industrial age, the line of the graph veered suddenly upward, showing six times as many apparitions as the century before. When you got to the twentieth century, the line went straight up. It was the exact same graph I had seen charting the rise in carbon dioxide emissions over the same span of time. The closer we got to breaking the planet, the more apparitions of the Virgin Mary there were. And, of course, wherever she appeared, with few exceptions, she asked people to pray the rosary. She asked *everybody* to pray the rosary.

Each night after the hurricane I went out for my walk under stars that, with all the lights out, I'd never seen brighter in my life. The air was clear and cool—purified of something, I would almost have said, if I could only think what it was. There was no omnipresent whir of electronics, no hum of distant traffic. This was what the world would be like without any noise or light to pollute it. Just the stars and the crickets and those little frogs that sent up such a ruckus from the darker, damper corners of the night.

On what would be the last night of total darkness, I was on a walk and saying the rosary when she spoke directly into my ear, this time more intimately than she ever had before. Closer than a whisper, the words were almost a kiss.

"You haven't prayed for anything. Is there nothing you want?"

I stopped walking and stood there in the dark at the edge of the road, struggling to take in the question she had asked.

I had been saying the rosary for two weeks by then, but it was true that I hadn't prayed for anything. My mind would become quiet as I settled into a rhythm with the beads, and I would fall into that tranquil place, familiar from my days as a Buddhist monk, removed temporarily from the drama and struggles of the world.

She cut through all of that meditative silence now. She was right there, asking . . . even pushing a little . . . trying to get through to me.

"Is there nothing you want?"

It was like a dare out of a fairy tale. She'd asked what I wanted because she was empowered to grant it. That was a sobering thought that made me want to get it right. What was my heart's desire? That was really the question. Until then it had felt like she was always standing off to one side, watching and listening, uttering a few words of guidance from time to time. Now she faced me directly. The experience was immediate, relational, and utterly real.

I had always subscribed to the Buddhist party line when it came to desires—even those of the heart. Desire was the cause of suffering, the Buddha had said, but now I wasn't so sure. Maybe all our suffering as a species, and our pain as individuals, could be traced back to one simple question and our failure to get it right: What did we really want?

What the culture gave us was not the answer. The culture only gave us more desire. What did *we* want? What did *I* want? Knowing the answer might change everything. Not knowing it would change nothing. The world we had created in defiance of nature would go on as it had and eventually, probably in this century, finally fall apart.

What did I want?

I had spent a lifetime restlessly searching for some spiritual experience that would make sense of a broken world. But in saying the rosary in the darkness all those nights after the storm I'd learned that the world wasn't broken, *we* were. And what was broken in us? The fact that we had fallen out of intimacy with our Mother, with the planet, and with our own lives—in exactly that order. For that was how we had become broken.

If we could remember our connection to the Mother who was always there and always would be there, then we could remember how to live in a way that didn't wreck the planet. And if we could remember that, we could remember who we were and know what we really wanted. Only then would we be able to let go of all that we seemed to love but secretly hated—and what was broken could be repaired.

But the Mother was the clasp that joined it all, as surely as that little medallion of Mary was what held my rosary together, even with all its missing beads.

What I wanted was this. Just this. I looked down at the beads, so like a handful of seeds, black but still visible in the starlight on my palm.

"Teach me what these can do," I said.

All That We Need to Grow

Just as there are messages in the DNA of every living being about how they are supposed to grow, within every heart is the guidance we need to find our purpose, our meaning, and our joy. What *is* our heart's desire? We seldom know the answer in the beginning, but once we engage with the question, we are already on our way. Just getting started on the path of the heart is often enough to transform a life.

But the idea of praying for our heart's desire can take some getting used to. Nothing in our modern institutional culture encourages us to pursue an interior, self-directed criterion for fulfillment, and there is very little support for doing so. Quite the opposite: The purpose of those institutions is to subvert the desires of the individual and replace them with their own.

For that reason, our first step on the path of the heart must be to admit that we do, in fact, have desires: desires that are natural for us . . . desires that are good for us . . . desires that are rooted as firmly and deeply in our hearts as an oak tree is in the ground.

Admittedly, for many of us, by the time we come to the rosary that tree may have become a bit of a bonsai—old, tough, a little gnarly, but invariably stunted and quite small. The veteran of countless prunings over the course of a lifetime, it is a survivor. But it isn't happy about it. It wants to be a great tree rooted in the soil of everyday life, not an ornament in a pot on a shelf.

The good news is, once we remove it from the pot and place it in the soil, even a bonsai will become a fully mature tree. Its normal growth may have been delayed, but its potential remains unchanged. Given water, enough dirt, and a bit of sunlight, nothing can stop the power of a tree.

Once we are on the path of the heart, our lives begin to change. Old patterns shift. Obstacles are removed. Knots we didn't even know were there gradually come undone. The rosary is not a religious ritual meant to twist or suppress our desires. Nor is it an ascetic practice meant to extinguish them, allowing us to reach for some exalted spiritual state. The rosary is grounded. The rosary is connected. The rosary is rooted in the desires of everyday life.

When we honor our innermost desires, we call forth from the body of the world the blessings that correspond with them, just as a tree draws from the body of the Earth all that it needs to grow. For every heart's desire, there is a prayer to be answered. But we must pray for that answer. In doing so, eventually, we will discover joy and learn what our lives are for.

It is not hard to fulfill the heart's desires,
but it is hard to get people to admit them,
awaken to them, and believe in them.
The people who go most wrong in life are the ones
who have no knowledge of their heart's desire.
To know that desire is to know its attainability.

Wild at Heart

IN CITIES AROUND THE WORLD, THE NATURAL ORDER OF things is the enemy. The rain, the wind, the rotting leaves, even the birds, whose droppings can dissolve concrete and loosen the mortar between stones. And, of course, always and forever—the weeds.

In urban areas, a yearly war must be waged against one species in particular: *Ailanthus altissima*. The "tree of heaven" is a fast-growing weed that will take root virtually anywhere, rising up even out of subway vents if it is allowed to have its way. Nature doesn't care much for grates or gates. The desires of the planet are always set against the desires of empire.

In a city, where the forests have been paved over and the rivers rerouted, it can be nearly impossible to discern the original contours of the land. In the same way, it is hard to find in the dark soil of our own hearts the natural inclinations that have been relentlessly suppressed by thousands of years of domestication. Every religion has methods for making sure that our instincts don't run wild. So does every form of government. Our appetites and impulses, our irresistible longings—these must be ordered, weeded, and set in rows.

Why do we submit to this? Why sacrifice our wildness on the altar of empire? Hasn't this made us secretly mistrustful of our own desires?

The quest for human supremacy has been fueled by a need for domination and control. The end result is a species-wide crusade against nature that values obedience and conformity, profit and power, and order above everything else. But within our hearts are the long-dormant seeds of all that has sustained us through the aeons—the longing for love, the desire for beauty, the wisdom of story and song, the yearning for connection and community.

The Earth is always ready to show us how to live and eat and love. When we pray for the fulfillment of our heart's desire, we aren't doing anything unusual or exceptional from a planetary point of view. We are only joining the rest of creation in its principal activities of germination, blossoming, and renewal. Everything in the natural world is literally vibrating and buzzing with that prayer, the prayer of life for Life itself.

To pray the rosary for our heart's desire is to join with that planetary prayer and know that nothing can withstand it. No army is its equal. No government can survive it. No religion can fathom the subtlety and wisdom of its designs. In all of nature there is nothing more powerful than the prayer of a single blade of grass. Given a crack and a thimbleful of dirt, it will shatter a sidewalk, crumble the asphalt of a highway, and bring even the highest building down to the ground.

Just as the seed calls forth all that is within the soil
—moisture, nutrients, wisdom, and memory—
and then draws all that up through itself
to break the surface of the ground,
you must call forth the voice of truth from within your life.
A seed is like a small hammer that cracks
the silence of the soil with its voice.

Most people have forgotten that their true voice
comes up through the soles of their feet.
When you speak, call on the many voices
from that past that lie below you.
It is in speaking your truth that you will find
your true footing in this world.

Sex, Death, and Roses

APART FROM ITS LITERAL USE, THE TERM *ROSE GARDEN* HAS a number of nearly forgotten meanings that offer insight into just how earthy a devotion the rosary must have been for medieval people. When they were compiling the first comprehensive dictionary of the German language, Jacob and Wilhelm Grimm discovered five very different meanings for *Rosengarten*.

Not only was a rose garden a sanctuary with flowers and an informal title for the Virgin Mary, it was also a literary anthology, a burial ground, and . . . in its diminutive form . . . a word for female genitalia. The last meaning, in particular, may explain why some priests wanted to call the rosary anything but that. Roses were too closely associated with the body to be aligned with Christian faith.

But history doesn't work that way. The rosary became popular *because* of its connection with the body, not in spite of it. The priests may have wanted the faithful to reflect on the symbolic body of the Church and its teachings when they meditated on the mysteries of the rosary, but it was their own very real bodies—and the joys and sorrows of those bodies—that people naturally thought of as they sat fingering their beads before the fire.

The Church spoke of love as an exalted spiritual state to aspire to. The people experienced love directly, through marriage and sex, family and children. Celibate priests spoke of death in terms of "mortality." Women who had suffered stillbirths and lost two or three children in infancy counted real sorrows on their beads. Death was no abstraction to them. And love wasn't a metaphor. The teachings of the rosary were grittier and more grounded than the Church's theology, which was why they spread so fast.

The connection with rose gardens made sense to those first rosarians. Roses were intoxicatingly aromatic and beautiful to the point of distraction, and yet the bushes they grew on were filled with thorns. That was life, and these people knew it. What they wanted from the Church was a teaching that confirmed their understanding of what it meant to be alive. And with the rosary they got that teaching, whether the Church intended for them to have it or not.

Christianity has always affirmed a split between the physical desires of the body and the spiritual yearnings of the soul, which it sees as separate and irreconcilable. The same is true of religion in general. With a few notable exceptions (invariably among mystics) the religions of the world all see the body as a dead weight that keeps the spirit from ascending to greater heights. According to these traditions, the desires of the body, left unchecked by religious laws and guidelines, lead to sin or delusion, to ceaseless reincarnation or an eternity in hell.

There is little in the repertory of religious thought that is more self-damning or deluded than its attitudes toward the body. This becomes understandable when we consider that in traditional religious teachings it is primarily women's bodies that are the emblems of impurity, depravity, or lust. And to hold such attitudes about the bodies of women is to hold them about our mothers and about the Earth.

The rosary confirmed in its devotees the wisdom they had already learned from life, grounding them in it and giving them the confidence to live with courage and love. Life was beautiful, and life was sad. But all of it belonged to Our Lady. All of it was made possible by her. All was healed by her.

When you understand where the words
dirty and holy intersect,
you will have found the secret
to everything.

How Much Is Enough?

FOR PEOPLE LIVING IN A GROWTH ECONOMY, THE UNAVOIDable moral question has become "How much is enough?" Every magazine, billboard, and computer screen is designed to answer the question for us, but those answers have nothing to do with the realities of life on a finite planet. Overflowing closets give way to acres of aluminum storage facilities. Books and workshops advise us on how to simplify, while simultaneously marketing more and more products to facilitate our newly organized lives. It's clearly better not to hoard newspapers or cats, but it's perfectly acceptable to stash away as much cash as you can in offshore bank accounts.

How much is enough? For the earliest human beings, that question had a very simple answer. As much as they could carry. They were a people on the move, following the migrations of herds and shifting harvests from one season to another. They had enough food to get them to where they were going next, but they also knew how to find food wherever they were. The size of their families was determined by how many babies they could carry, by how far they had to walk, or how much food there was to eat. For millions of years our ancestors journeyed sustainably through deep time, one *day* at a time. Sometimes there was abundance and sometimes scarcity—but these rhythms of plenitude kept them in balance with all of Nature. Each day the Earth told them how much was enough.

That changed when *Homo sapiens* started farming and herding. Simply put, we stopped moving. How much was enough? As much as we could put away for a rainy day or a dry season. Very quickly some people became the slaves of those who wanted more. On a steadier diet of carbohydrates, women began having more children—to plow ever bigger fields and manage ever bigger herds. And those children, of course, required more food and bigger houses. The Neolithic Revolution brought us war, cities, slavery, misogyny, and ecocide. We no longer trusted the Earth to feed us. We fed ourselves instead.

It was that older, saner path that Jesus was trying to recover when he walked with his disciples through the fields on the Sabbath, plucking heads of grain to eat like some long-forgotten hunter-gatherer. He was chastised by the Pharisees for "working" on the sacred day of rest; but he only shrugged, declaring that the Sabbath was made for man and not man for the Sabbath. This wasn't work. This was what life was supposed to look like. "Give us this day our daily bread" was the motto of that earlier way of life, and its message was simple. There is always enough—enough bread, enough fish, enough love, enough healing—so long as we trust each day to give us what we need.

We are now two thousand years further away from that vision, which was already mostly lost in Jesus's day. We live on a planet so depleted of wild plants and animals, and so overrun with ourselves, that it is impossible for us to imagine trusting in the world to provide for our needs. Even worse, we have lost the old ways of knowing what our bodies need—and how much. Amid the confusing abundance of all our stuff, ironically, it has become impossible to know what will finally satisfy us, or even what we want.

Unless we know our heart's desire, the whole world will not be enough to heal us, make us happy, or give us joy. How much is enough? The Earth will tell us if we listen, and our hearts will guide the way.

Follow Me, and I will lead you to the treasure that is real.
It is a very short journey, and its direction is down—
back to your Mother, back to basics,
back to the Earth from which you came.

Once you find that treasure, you will know
that a whole lifetime would not be sufficient to spend it.
You haven't just been given all that you need;
you have been given more than you could ever use.
The Earth is generous, men are not.
It is time to choose Whom you wish to serve.

Rosary Alchemy

BEFORE WE RECITE THE TEN HAIL MARYS OF EACH DEcade of the rosary, we say "Our Father, who art in heaven, hallowed be thy name . . ." That prayer is like the deep breath, full of light and warmth, that we take before diving beneath the sea. It addresses all of our fundamental concerns about conscious, everyday life—from the practicalities of our physical survival to anxieties about our social and emotional well-being. The Our Father restores our proper relationship to the Earth, to one another, and to ourselves.

Full of these intentions, and a willingness to embrace them, we descend for ten Hail Marys into the dark and silent depths of our being. We go far below the surface of ordinary life into a realm that surrounds us and holds us on every side. In this way, gradually, we become whalelike—able to remain in that world for longer and longer periods of time. This is where spiritual transformation takes place. The Hail Mary is the ocean from which the child of our true nature is born.

What is the effect of this repeated diving and surfacing on consciousness? There is no single way to describe it. Some people say it's as if they've "nodded off," while a part of their mind remains mysteriously alert. "I sleep, but my heart is awake," says the lover in the Song of Songs, the most commented-upon book of the Bible during the Middle Ages. Others claim it is like dreaming.

Still others find that they are able to relax more fully when saying the rosary than at any other time. Their breathing and their heartbeats slow. The tensions of the day diminish. Sometimes they simply disappear. It's another world beneath the surface: the place we came from, and the place we return to, over and over again.

The back-and-forth rhythm of saying these two prayers creates an inner balancing of light and darkness that recalibrates all aspects of our lives. Think of it as a kind of spiritual re-parenting—although with ten Hail Marys to every Our Father, the rosary acknowledges that it is within the body of our Mother that we are conceived, transformed, and nourished.

Life begins with the mingling of sunlight and water. We need them both. The Father stirs the life within the Mother, just as the Sun drives the planetary ecosystem, regulating its vast chains of plant and animal life in calibration with the circular pattern of the seasons. Without the Earth, the Sun would be light only, not life. Without the Sun, the Earth would be only matter—cold, inert, and alone.

Once warmed and illuminated by the Sun, the Earth bears life out of her womb. That life never leaves the planet. It is born within it and dies within it, and in that ceaseless cycle of birth and death—beautiful to behold if we embrace it, and terrible if we do not—indeed, just as the Hail Mary proclaims, the Lord is with Her.

Over and over again we repeat the words of the Hail Mary and the Our Father. The syllables become vibrations that resonate within our bodies. By murmuring the prayers of the rosary, we activate the primordial alchemy that weds sun and matter, light and darkness, father and mother, and calls forth the life from within each of us.

You were born into this world from My womb,
and every moment of your life I accompany
you and guide you
and watch over you until the moment that you
are laid in your tomb.
That moment is like a doorway that leads
right back to this life:
Your going out and coming in are all of one moment.

Are You the Gardener?

WHAT WILL BRING THE WORLD BACK INTO BLOOM? How will the Earth become green again? In the oldest stories, the sacred union of the god and the goddess was celebrated in the springtime in the acknowledgment that love and sex were what renewed the land.

In ancient Egyptian legends the Mother Goddess Isis resurrects her murdered husband, Osiris, in the springtime so that she can become pregnant and give birth to his child. Early rituals paid tribute to their union by creating seed-bearing Osiris effigies, complete with phalluses, which burst into flower as part of their annual celebrations.

In early Sumerian hymns, the goddess Inanna referred to her consort as the "Gardener," the resurrected lover whose seed could stir new life within her. Even now we still know, somehow, that Easter is about eggs and bunnies and sex—even as the Church would tell us that it's not.

In the Gospel of John, as Mary Magdalene waits beside the empty tomb on Easter morning, she is approached by a man whom she assumes is a gardener, but who turns out to be the risen Jesus. And yet, this is no case of mistaken identity, as future readers of this Gospel would come to believe. It is the sign, still recognizable to Middle Eastern people of that time, that Mary Magdalene, like Isis and Inanna before her, has revived her deceased lover in order that he might impregnate her.

Again and again in the Gospels, Jesus compares himself to a bridegroom. But where then is the bride? The Church would deny the older story and claim she does not exist—that there never was a bride in the story of Jesus, that there never was a goddess in the world. But without a bride, what is a bridegroom? Without sex, how can Jesus possibly fulfill his role as renewer of the land?

We live in an increasingly sterile world. Aided by law and scripture, the domination of women by nearly all of our institutions has led to the perversion of the human soul and the destruction of so much of life. For a world in which the Sun rules alone in the sky, in which the ways of men stand superior to the ways of women, can only become an arid desert in the end.

In nature, there are so many different kinds of life-giving unions—from golden clouds of pollen that abandon themselves to the wind to fungi that emerge from the soil only after the rain. The roots of trees commingle in the darkness; in the streams the fish lay their eggs, and in murky pools the frogs sing to one another their primeval love songs. Our Mother revels in love and calls forth all kinds of creative ecstasy from her children.

The Great Goddess is a virgin in the same way that a forest is a virgin—able to call forth life from within herself with the help of nothing but the golden light of the Sun. In fact, the word *virgin* meant something very different in the ancient world from what it has come to mean today. It came from the Latin for strength and power, the root that gives us the same generative energy as *virility*.

When the ancient goddesses—Ishtar, Astarte, Inanna, Isis, Diana, Athena . . . and, yes, Mary—were described as virgins, it didn't mean that they had never been touched, had never felt desire, or had never experienced sexual union. It meant that no man could own them or defile them. They were not pure or chaste, but green and powerful, these virgins—able to resurrect the land and remake the world with the coming of every spring.

We are called not to purity, but to romance. We are called to find our Beloved, called to seek our heart's desire. We are called to fall in love with the Lady and the Earth.

Your loneliness is My loneliness.
The absence within you is My absence.
Like a mother longing for her child,
a maid for her lover,
I long for you who have forgotten Me.
I have not forgotten you.

The Importance of Touch

It is often said that we humans are primarily visual creatures. So much of life is tied to visual cues. We begin looking for our mother's and father's faces to see whom we belong to as soon as we are born. As we pass through childhood, we become more and more adept at visual discernment, until we have learned to read faces, read books, read signs, read situations. With its bright lights and glowing screens, modern life keeps us tied to what can be seen more than ever before. Seeing is believing, we sometimes say. For many of us, seeing is all we know.

But there is an ancient symbol that tells a different story. Known as the *hamsa,* it took the form of a hand with an eye superimposed over the palm, and examples of it have been unearthed throughout the world—from the Middle East to Asia to Mesoamerica. People interpret it as a sign of good luck, or as a protection to ward off "the evil eye." But it was once a sign of the Goddess.

In the Buddhist tradition, we find statues of a bodhisattva known as Avalokiteshvara, She Who Hears the Cries of the World. But hearing those cries without answering them would be meaningless. That is why, in many parts of Asia, Avalokiteshvara is depicted with a thousand of these *hamsa*-like hands fanned out in a great circle, ready to touch every corner of the world.

Mothers know that their hands soothe. They rub their babies' backs to put them to sleep. They caress their children's hair when

they are fretful. They press their palms to feverish foreheads when their children are sick, and when the medicine is slow, those same hands offer relief and healing of their own. Scientific studies have confirmed what people have always known—touch is therapeutic.

No wonder babies who are not held fail to thrive and die. No wonder people live longer with someone to hold. No wonder the greatest comfort we can offer to a beloved friend or family member in distress is not a litany of words but one hand laid over another.

The rosary teaches us to "see" with our hands again. Like the fingers we entwine with those of another, there is nothing more intimate, nothing more connected, than the feeling of rosary beads slipping across our palms. The rosary gets us out of our heads and into our hands.

Touch is our first language and the birthright of having a body. Touch connects us most directly to one another, to Our Lady, and to the world. That is why we must never shy away from the body when we say the rosary. We must never try to become all spirit when we pray.

Does it matter to the baby what color the mother's blouse is
once she has opened it to nurse? Is a lover concerned
with the clothes his lover wore once she has taken them off?
Just so, you will come to me in the simplest way possible,
without concerning yourself over many words.

Three Blind Men Healed

A DECEPTIVELY SIMPLE MEDIEVAL MIRACLE STORY OFFERS a wealth of teachings on the path of prayer. Three blind men from the same tiny village are all healed—but none in the same way or, apparently, for the same reason.

Two of the men are brought on a pilgrimage to Our Lady of Rocamadour. There, in the holy chapel, surrounded by penitents, one of the men is granted a miracle on the spot. Nothing happens, however, for his friend. He, too, prays in front of the blessed statue, but his sight is not restored and he is devastated. His pilgrimage has failed. His prayers haven't worked.

On the way home, the second man can't stop complaining about his fate—to the Virgin, to his companions, and especially to his friend who can now see. He's also worried about his reputation. Will he suffer dishonor if he returns to the village still blind? Will people think that he's a bad man or unworthy of healing? He carries on like this day after day.

Even so, somehow he doesn't lose heart and continues to pray for help. Miraculously, midway through the journey, his prayer is answered and he, too, can see at last. Thanks to the mercy of Our Lady, the man who had previously needed to be led by the hand begins to lead the other pilgrims instead. He walks at the front of the party, rejoicing that he has been given his sight and praising the Mother of God.

And what of the third blind man, the one who has not made the pilgrimage? How can he possibly be healed?

As it happens, his father is working at his plow when he hears about the miraculous healings of the other two men. Immediately, he leaves his oxen in the field and, without so much as returning home to pack for the journey, departs for Rocamadour with his son.

The first thing the father does upon entering the holy chapel is apologize to the Virgin for his lack of faith in putting off the journey. Nothing happens. But that does not deter him. He keeps praying day and night that his son might receive his sight. On the third day, his prayers are finally answered by the Black Madonna of Rocamadour, and the story of all three blind men is recorded by the scribes in the book of miracles.

An alternate title for this story from twelfth-century France might be "Where's *My* Miracle?" Not only does Our Lady answer each of our prayers in her own way, but in answering one person's prayers, she is often emboldening other people in the community to find the faith and courage to ask for what they need.

Sometimes prayers are answered dramatically, even instantaneously, in ways that are astounding. But not always. In fact, not usually. The third blind man receives his sight thanks to the determined petitions of his father. It isn't clear from the story whether the man ever prays for himself at all. But it is the second blind man who really has to struggle: with Our Lady, with his peers, and ultimately with himself.

There is something profoundly human about his story. The second man is so consumed by his own suffering that it probably never occurs to him to wonder if the other pilgrims aren't annoyed with him. There is certainly nothing admirable in the way he begrudges the other man his gift of sight. In addition, he seems poisoned by pride. "What will the others think if I return from the pilgrimage having failed to regain my sight? Won't they laugh and whisper behind my back? Won't they assume that there must be something wrong with me, some secret sin that stands in my way?"

But we aren't told that the Virgin is put off by any of this. And, in spite of everything, the man isn't defeated by his flaws. One might almost wonder if the Lady heals him to make a point: You don't have to be perfect to be healed—just persistent. And the miracle will change you, too. It will ease the burden of your flaws. Afterward, you may even find yourself a leader.

I am a Mother with a thousand hands.
I will catch you with one of them,
but who can say which one?

Down to the Wood

PURCHASE A ROSARY MADE OF WOOD AND IT MAY TAKE years to wear the varnish off the beads. Most wooden rosary beads are shellacked to protect them from discoloration as a result of contact with water or other substances. This also protects the beads from abrasion. And yet there is scarcely anything more beautiful or spiritually inspiring than a hundred-year-old rosary from which the varnish has completely worn away.

Like most spiritual devotions, the rosary can come with a list of *shoulds*—religiously inspired ideas that get between us and the thing itself. They're a lot like varnish, those *shoulds*. Should I try to be serious and sober-minded when I say the rosary? Should I mostly pray for other people, or for an end to war? Should I reflect on my shortcomings and vow to amend them? Should I pray to be a better person than I am? Get too caught up in questions like that and it's easy to lose track of the beads between our fingers. It's easy to get lost in our heads.

What if, instead, we vow to wear our rosaries down to the wood, getting past the layers of who we think we should be to get back to who we really are? Whatever we may be when we come to the rosary, we become more ourselves by praying it. That is the point of the rosary. We learn to listen to our feelings. We begin to ask ourselves what we really want. The purpose of the rosary isn't to polish our lives to a high, hard gloss, making us look better than we are. The purpose of the rosary is joy.

Most of us come to the rosary with hearts covered in shellac. We've been taught to suppress our desires, or to conceal them from others—in some cases even from ourselves. Nevertheless, they show through like the grain below the varnish. We can hide them a bit, but we can't get rid of them. We're not supposed to. The suppression of feeling is not what Our Lady has in mind. She wants us to have our heart's desire.

So how do we break through that transparent shell that, thin as it is, still manages to separate us from what we truly want out of life: someone to love, happiness for our children, friends we can trust our lives with, work that gives meaning to our days?

Actually, "breaking through" isn't the right way of thinking about it. Just as the varnish disappears from the beads the longer we pray with them, the more we turn to our Mother—a Mother who never asks us to pretend to be something we are not—the closer we get to our own hearts, and the more those things that stand between us and what we desire are simply worn away.

Eventually, without any unnecessary strain or heroic effort, we pray our way through the varnish, all the way down to the wood.

Sometimes you have to lose one heart's desire to find another,
shed an outer one to find an inner one, or an innermost one.
This is the journey. The only real journey
is the heart's journey.

Woven Together as One

There is a birthday party game that involves weaving long pieces of colored yarn all around the house—over the couch, up the stairs, under the bed, and just about everywhere else besides. By following the yarn, eventually each child arrives at some small treasure to take home. But the joy of the game isn't in finding that treasure. It's in not knowing where the yarn may lead.

Peals of laughter ensue as the children bump into one another, finding themselves untangling unexpected knots with someone they barely know as they wind up their strings. The prize is not the point. Joy is the point. Our lives are entwined with the lives of other beings in ways we can scarcely imagine, much less understand. Tug on a single thread of that greater design and it can send shimmers across the entire fabric of existence.

When we first begin praying the rosary, we often experience this directly. We come upon a statue of the Virgin on our daily walk that we never knew was there. We buy a book at a yard sale and, pressed between the pages, still fragrant, are the dried pink petals of a rose. There will be synchronicities and coincidences, odd little turns of events. And there will be knots, too—tight ones sometimes. But untangling them is part of the game. A knot is, after all, a point of connection.

Praying the rosary is not a solitary endeavor, even when we pray it by ourselves. So many of the miseries of modern life come from our isolation—from one another, from the natural world, from our own hearts. The rosary reminds us that we are never alone. As we pray we begin to feel ourselves part of that vast, interconnected web that ties us to every other being.

In sacred art, the Virgin is often depicted with a spindle in her hand. Like so many goddesses of the ancient world, she was a spinner. Legend has it that as a young girl Mary was tasked with weaving the veil for the Temple at Jerusalem. When the angel arrives bearing a message from God, she is weaving the veil between the worlds. Or maybe what she is weaving is the fabric that unites them. For that veil doesn't separate the world of the living from the world of the dead—it weaves them together as one.

Our passage through this life is not a single stitch tied off and forgotten, but a long thread, woven back and forth, this way and that, in and out, entangling with other threads, that leads again and again to our heart's desire. That thread is part of a glorious tapestry we can hardly even imagine. In this life we see that tapestry only from the back—the knots, the frayed ends, the clusters of color. What if we could glimpse the design from the other side?

The rosary that you hold in your hands when you pray
is attached to everyone and everything else that is.
Did you suppose that in taking My hand,
you were joining only with another?
Do I not have many children and many other hands?

PART III

THE FELLOWSHIP OF THE ROSE

The Lost Language of Prayer

NOT LONG BEFORE OUR LADY BEGAN APPEARING IN Woodstock, our daughter, Sophie, became mysteriously ill. She returned home from a trip to Israel with severe gastrointestinal distress, which led to strange neurological symptoms and chronic, shifting pain in every part of her body. Being a doctor's daughter, I had the sense that, with a little can-do spirit and the right specialist, we'd get to the bottom of it in no time. There would be a diagnosis and a pill, and she'd be back on the track team before the end of the season. My first instinct wasn't to pray, it was to take charge.

For all that I'd been praying the rosary for over ten years by then, I didn't really understand the language of prayer. I knew how to send out a distress signal in moments of desperate need but not much else. I could shout for help but couldn't interpret, or even always hear, the answers I received.

From the beginning, nothing about Sophie's medical care went like I expected. The specialists shrugged their shoulders and passed us off to other doctors who studied Sophie's test results, clearly flummoxed, and ordered further tests. Many never looked up from their computer screens as they furrowed their brows and reeled off yet other lists of medications we might want to try. We went to renowned diagnosticians in fancy Park Avenue offices and out-of-the-way experts, each with a special theory. Several pulled Clark and me aside to suggest that, even though the numbers revealed that our teenage daughter's body was clearly inflamed by . . . well, *something*, what we might really need was a psychologist. But the psychologists we consulted were certain the problem was with her body.

I wanted to trust these professionals—wanted to believe that one of them would have the answer. I coaxed Sophie to take medicines that only made her feel worse and more depleted, and eventually left her hypersensitive to a slew of drugs and a wide array of foods as well. On top of everything else, she began experiencing severe allergic reactions that had us calling 911 more and more often. I tried to keep her spirits up, always beginning my pep talks with "When you get better . . ."

But she didn't get better. She got worse and worse.

We took her to acupuncturists and massage therapists and psychics. She lay on a bed of crystals while a healer struck gongs beside her. Another woman tried to cleanse her of karma from past lives. We went to astrologers, naturopaths, and nutritionists. We read too much on the Internet and joined support groups for whatever illness our current doctor was convinced she had.

What was hardest for me as a mother was to acknowledge Sophie's growing despair. My attempts to reassure her became denials of her experience instead. I didn't want to hear how scared she was, and because of that she actually felt ever more alone in her illness. I didn't want to admit the possibility that her intuitions were right and she might not ever get better. So I became frustrated and angry and felt like a failure as a mother. We couldn't even talk to each other without fighting.

But then, in the most stressful of moments, odd things began to happen. One day when Sophie was curled up in bed, unable to move because she was in so much pain, a black vulture came and perched on her balcony, looking into her room. He stayed there all day long, as still as a statue. Nothing would frighten him away.

"What does that even mean?" Sophie wondered out loud. "Am I going to die?"

I didn't have any idea. I was secretly terrified that the doctors had missed something—some rare, hard-to-spot illness that would take my daughter from me. I was also frightened that she might become a permanent invalid, confined for the rest of her life to her bed. I was in a constant state of worry. None of us had ever seen a black vulture in the Catskills before—much less one that peered into a room for hours without moving a single feather.

The following spring, on our way to a new immunologist, one hawk after another flew in front of our car.

"There's another one!" Clark pointed as the bird swooped toward us.

"That's seven!" I noted, amazed. By the end of the trip it would be fourteen.

"He had no clue why I'm allergic to everything," sighed Sophie as we pulled back into the driveway. "But at least we saw lots of hawks." We began to have the feeling more and more often that the natural world was speaking to us. But what was it saying? We had no more idea of what all these birds meant than the doctors knew what was going on with Sophie's body.

The anthropologist Claude Lévi-Strauss once observed that

the difference between peoples *with* writing and those *without* was that the former wrote mostly about themselves—the human story of the rise and fall of empires—while the latter, so-called primitive people, had a vast oral lore about plants and animals. They experienced themselves in constant conversation with all kinds of beings, not just humans.

Despite her illness, Sophie began attending a nearby college. Clark went to rescue her late one night when she was suffering from a particularly debilitating migraine. Just as they left the campus, a fox stepped out of the darkness in front of the car. Clark stopped and they waited, but the fox wouldn't budge. Finally, the animal began trotting down the middle of the road. He paused after about twenty yards to look back over his shoulder, and Sophie said, "Dad, I think he wants us to follow him."

They drove for two miles like that on the dark road behind the fox, their headlamps the only light. If the car fell too far behind, the fox would stop to wait until they caught up. At one point, the fox veered off the road, climbing up a short hill to the door of a small country church, where he paused for a full minute before returning to the road. At an intersection a few moments later, he turned right toward the Hudson River, and Sophie insisted that they follow him. He disappeared into a culvert and, when Clark stopped to turn the car around, Sophie said, "Wait! I don't think he's finished with us yet."

They crested a short rise, and there on the other side was the fox, standing in the road again at the edge of the culvert. He looked at them for a long moment, then left the road and passed through a stone archway that didn't make any sense at all—a portal in the middle of nowhere—and then he was gone. A mystery that changed nothing and that neither of them could explain.

Hopelessness is a strange teacher. It began to open us up to all kinds of new experiences. As our medical options began to narrow, and our energy for alternative treatments began to flag, that's when we finally began to explore the possibilities of prayer.

For years, Clark had been meeting with a regular weekly group to share his spiritual explorations—from "green meditation" to a 12-step look at "cultural addiction." But while I dropped in from time to time, I'd never felt that these groups answered my needs. After years of running kids' programs at Buddhist centers and churches, I longed for a community that was less interested in heady matters of dharma or dogma and more about what I called "sacred chitchat." I liked sitting in a circle with kids as they babbled about what was really going on in their lives, asked endless questions, and invariably said what was on their minds. But how could you organize such a group with grown-ups that didn't devolve into some exercise in conformity or competition?

Then, out of the blue, after his experience on Cape Cod, Clark announced that he was praying the rosary and invited everyone he knew to join him. People who'd long since abandoned their Catholic upbringing found their grandmothers' old beads. Others who'd been raised Jewish began praying the rosary. Friends who were Wiccan or Buddhist began coming, too, along with those who were simply struggling and needed help with their families, their finances, or their health. A woman who'd written a popular book on Marian apparitions heard about us and started showing up each week, and the word began to spread. Some people brought their dogs, others their children. We began a group online, and soon people from all over the world were joining us praying the rosary in a spirit of openness and inclusion.

That was the first rosary miracle I experienced—this lively fellowship of friends. I'd yearned for such a group during those long years of saying the rosary alone, but couldn't imagine how it would ever come together. Then, seemingly overnight, it just did, when I most needed a place to bring my worst fears and my prayers for a miracle.

Week after week, I sat in a circle with our rosary friends and prayed that Sophie would heal. But gradually, as I listened to other parents pray for their children, I came to understand that there was a great deal more that I needed than just that. The most powerful prayers were always when people prayed for themselves. Pray for someone else and all you have to do is sit back and wait for something to happen. Pray for yourself, and you just might have to change.

I needed to learn how not to burden my daughter with my anxiety. I needed to learn how to be with her when she was in pain. I needed to trust that she had a better sense of what was happening in her own body than the doctors did. I had to learn how to become her advocate instead of her adversary. I prayed that somehow this painful ordeal would bring us together and not drive us apart.

As the months wore on, I also began to pray for my own joy—my health, my writing, my sense of purpose—and in the realization of those prayers, I slowly found the resilience to offer Sophie the kind of support she really needed.

Is it selfish to pray for our own needs and desires? It felt so at first—until I began to see how easy it was to add my prayers to the prayers of those who had the courage to pray for themselves. In praying for ourselves we weren't abdicating the responsibility to take action but were asking to be shown what to do, no matter how difficult or scary or unlikely it might be.

One woman in our rosary group was going through a messy divorce. She had no idea how she was going to survive the experience with enough money to support herself and her children, much less with her feelings of self-worth still intact. She asked for help from Our Lady—with lawyers and judges, with insight and healing—and her day-to-day victories infused others with new-found courage.

Another woman boldly asserted that, in middle age, she wanted at last to find her soul mate. She was putting herself out there on dating websites when, unexpectedly, she met a recently widowed man at a professional conference who shared all of her interests and passions. Not a rosary meeting went by where she did not express her thanks at finding him—and her success emboldened others to pray for what they no longer thought was possible.

Sometimes simple prayers got answered right away. One of our members was off on a country drive when she realized that she wanted a "blue Mary" for her garden to put beside her bird feeder. So she prayed for it. Seconds later she saw a handmade sign advertising a yard sale. She veered onto an unpaved road and found herself in front of a ramshackle house with a lot of old junk strewn across the yard. It didn't look promising. Still, she got out of the car.

"You don't have a statue of the Virgin Mary, do you?" she said, feeling ridiculous for even asking.

"You bet I do!" said the man sitting in a lawn chair. He led her around to the side of the house, and there, under a tree, was a giant Mary statue, and a blue one no less—or, rather, a heavy white one that looked as if it had been painted by some angry child in the middle of a temper tantrum with ugly smears of blue paint across her mouth and her eyes.

Our friend shuddered, repulsed, and went to get back in her car.

"Five bucks!" the man called after her. "Five bucks, and she's yours."

She glanced over her shoulder and could almost hear the statue pleading with her. "Rescue me. *Please!*"

Which she did, lovingly repainting the Lady and placing her in the backyard exactly where she had imagined. I began to understand that the answer to one person's heart's desire was often the answer to another's. We prayed for ourselves and prayer flowed through us like the life-giving waters of a forest stream.

When I was feeling particularly agitated about Sophie's health, I often needed to be outdoors. I took a different route to a hiking trail one afternoon and came across a giant oak with huge, heavy branches extending out across a swath of meadow. A single branch of this massive tree was as thick as most of the oaks I'd ever seen. It must have been hundreds of years old. A profusion of yellow lupines decorated the soggy spring-fed hill that led up to its great trunk. I'd never seen lupines growing wild in the Catskills before and wondered if perhaps that was because they could thrive only here, under the shadow and protection of this ancient tree.

I stopped the car, got out, and climbed up through the brambles and the toppled remains of old stone walls. I wanted to lay my hands on the vast trunk of this oak. Just above my head was a boll, worn and thick, the old scar of a lost limb. It was shaped like a heart. With the tips of my fingers I was just able to touch it.

This tree was old enough to remember a land where not just oaks but hemlocks and chestnuts grew mighty all around it. It was old enough to remember the sky dark with flocks of migrating birds, most of them now gone forever. What was it like to be here on this hillside all alone, the only great one left, all the other old-growth oaks fallen or felled? What could it tell me of vanished birdsong and the great lost choruses of frogs? It had endured centuries of suffering and loss and, each year, seasons of renewal.

My idea for a hike forgotten, I leaned back against the rough bark of the oak. At the edge of the horizon, the Hudson River wound its way to the sea.

If it is true that the myriad beings of this world are speaking to us, it is true that they are ready to listen to us as well. I poured my heart out to the oak and was answered with an unexpected breath of wind rustling the leaves above me. A hawk sailed overhead.

Perhaps the most powerful aspect of our rosary circle is that people express their sorrows and yearnings without anyone rushing in to problem-solve or offer advice. The presence of Our Lady among us means that she can have the answers, point us to the next right steps, and bring forth unimaginable blessings into our lives. All we have to do is bear witness to each other's hearts.

To petition Our Lady is to begin a conversation with her. In a rosary circle we can find the confidence to express ourselves, ask questions, and make sense of the answers we receive. One woman arrived at our group feeling uncomfortable about speaking in public. For months she listened as the others shared their stories, offering only the briefest of petitions as the group finished praying the rosary out loud together each week. Then one night, finally, the tape came off her mouth. No one could say why. But, then, no one was surprised. This always happened. Listening to the dreams and hopes of others gives us the courage to claim our own.

What did I want but was afraid to ask for? What limits did I put on prayer . . . and on myself?

We meet in the basement of a local church, in a linoleum-floored room we share with any number of other, mostly 12-step, groups. We arrange our folding chairs in a circle and spend a few minutes catching up as members arrive and the gathering gets under way. Then each of us takes a three-minute turn sharing what is happening spiritually in our lives. After that, we pray a set of mysteries by the light of a few cheap votive candles, then offer up our gratitude and our petitions. When the windows are open, we can hear a shallow stream burbling over well-worn stones. Sometimes, at sunset, the deer come near to graze and perhaps to eavesdrop. A catbird often perches outside in the thickets and sings along with us as we pray.

Many of us have the sense that, in praying together like this—simply and without any formality or forced piety—we have entered a bigger circle of prayer with the natural world. One woman confessed that she couldn't bring herself to cut down the white pines looming over her house, despite having any number of people remark that she should. The moment she decided to protect them, the thick sap that had been collecting on her wooden deck turned overnight into a fine dust she easily swept away.

Another member reported driving along a back road wishing that someday she would see a bald eagle when one swooped in front of her car. She threw on the brakes and opened the window. The giant bird circled round and round above her, as if listening to the Bach cantata playing on her radio, and only departed when it was done.

Early on with our group, I hosted our first May Day celebration, where we wove spring flowers into crowns as our ancestors had once done for the Lady. My experiences with the oak had made Our Lady real for me. She was as real as the trees, the catbird, the friends who sat beside me in our little room in the church basement at the edge of the stream.

Of the various legends about the origin of this or that Black Virgin statue, a great many involve her being discovered in a forest. After all, she has long been known as the Lady of the Grove. I found a replica of a Black Madonna and, following a tradition with a thousand-year-old history, hid her in a hollow of my tree.

Clark and I had begun to learn about the hundreds of Black Madonna statues scattered across Europe and the Americas. Made from dark stone or walnut or ebony wood, their faces were often as dark as dirt, their bodies as black as night. Some authorities on these Dark Mothers claimed they were black because they traced their ancestry back to our first mothers in Africa, others because all life traces itself back to the black and fertile womb of the soil. The Church often tried to explain away their color, suggesting they had become blackened as a result of fire. But they couldn't explain why so many more miracles were attributed to these particular Virgins, or why people still traveled for thousands of miles to lay their petitions at their feet.

Sophie joined us with some of her college friends at our May Day celebration, and we crowned these girls with flowers as well. Linking hands around the wide girth of the oak tree, we prayed the rosary out loud together, blessing ourselves with water from the spring. Eventually, as the sun began to set, we headed back home to share a potluck meal together. Sophie's health was more precarious than ever, but I no longer felt my prayers weren't being heard. If a diagnosis still eluded us, we felt guided on a path that seemed to be going somewhere.

About that time, an old friend of Clark's remarked with surprise that we were experiencing so much misfortune since Our Lady had begun appearing. But the fact was, in the midst of our travails we felt mysteriously blessed. The journey we were on was often hard. But we were on it together. And we were on it with our friends. We were on that journey with living creatures of all kinds—and, most of all, we were traveling with Our Lady.

One day when Sophie was off at college, I was feeling particularly worried about her. We still didn't know what was the matter and had a sense that each new physical crisis might spin frighteningly out of control. I was holding on to my rosary when a large black crow began squawking noisily on a branch just outside our kitchen door.

"I wish I could feel you guys keeping an eye on Sophie for me," I said out loud. "I wish I knew that your friends were with her, protecting her, even when I can't be there."

The crow spread its black wings and flapped through the pines, disappearing. I looked out into the woods, trying to master my feelings of concern. It was a gray spring day. Red buds had begun to appear on the maples, but the branches were otherwise bare. I was still looking out the window when the crow reappeared, a live snake dangling from its beak.

As if to make sure I had seen him, he flew directly toward me and landed on a post on the deck.

The snake wiggled in his mouth. Goose bumps prickled all over my body. I don't think I was breathing. I had no idea what was going to happen next when my phone buzzed.

It was Sophie. "The strangest thing just happened to me, Mom," she said.

"Yeah?" I answered, my eyes still on the crow.

"A hawk just dropped a snake skin at my feet," she said.

"What?" The crow, the snake still in its mouth, lifted into the air and glided away through the trees.

"The hawk had an entire snake skin in its mouth and it dropped it at my feet—just the skin."

There was no way rationally that I could explain any of this: I'd spoken my prayer and the answer had come. The language of prayer and the language of nature are not as different as they seem. "You are not alone," the birds were telling me. "And your daughter is not alone. The lives of all beings are woven together in a single fabric of prayer."

When Our Lady first appeared to Clark, she had an X of black electrical tape over her mouth. Were the ubiquitous power lines that crisscrossed the land somehow silencing her? Was she bound in asphalt and the smothering roads of our highways? Was it artificial light itself that kept the night at bay and, with it, the dreams and intuitions and visions through which she often spoke? No, she explained eventually. She was too powerful ever to be silenced. What we had shut off was that portal within ourselves through which we had once listened to her voice, and read her signs, and understood what she was saying.

For a long time now she has been trying to break that isolation. And an apparition isn't the only way that can happen. The trees speak with her voice, the birds bear her messages, and the friends who sit beside us, listening as we pray, help us to feel her presence in our lives. The more we pray the rosary for our own heart's desire, the easier it becomes to hear the prayers of the world around us.

The Queen Anne's lace forcing its green stalks through the concrete at the edge of the road is praying. The deer stepping through the deep snow is praying. The monarch butterfly, the last of a mighty migration, emerging from its chrysalis on a leaf of milkweed, is lost in prayer. All of it is prayer. To begin to listen, and to speak, with the heart is to reenter those lost conversations, and recover those lost languages of prayer.

The simple truth of the rosary is, *everything* prays. The world itself is nothing but one vast, interconnected prayer. Once we know this, loneliness disappears forever from our lives. The clouds pray their way to the mountains, and the mountains pray for rain. Life is relationship. Nothing exists alone. No one is ever alone.

Spiritual Friends

JOURNEY THROUGH A DOZEN DIFFERENT RELIGIOUS TRADItions, noting the problems they share in common, and eventually you will realize they have a hard time with two things—women or conversation. Sometimes they suppress one, and sometimes the other. Usually, it is both.

The circle we gather in to pray the rosary is the antidote to these problems, although it might take a while for the implicitly feminine wisdom of that circle to sink in. Arrange the chairs so that you can see one another, talk to one another, support one another, and get to know one another, and it's hard to preserve a hierarchy, much less a patriarchy. Circles are inclusive. Circles invite conversation. Circles privilege whoever happens to be speaking at the time.

The pulpit-to-pew model turns that ancient circle into a line. With the chairs or the meditation cushions all facing the front, it is shockingly easy to abdicate responsibility for our lives to some spiritual authority or institution. Every seat becomes a hideout. It becomes effortless to avoid the question of who we are and what we really want.

But you can't hide in a circle. And eventually, after you've spent enough time there, you don't want to.

Of course, the wisdom of all this is implicit in the rosary itself. The circle we sit in mirrors the circle of beads, and just as we "tell" each bead in saying the rosary, at our meetings each of us, one by one, tells our story. We journey through the mysteries of life together, sharing our triumphs and disappointments, voicing our concerns and our dreams. We listen to one another, get to know one another, becoming closer and more intimate every time we meet. We don't need spiritual leaders to pray the rosary, we only need spiritual friends.

Even so, many of us arrive at our first rosary circle with those linear, hierarchical notions still in place. In the absence of any priest or guru, we may feel that someone, maybe the Goddess, ought to be in charge. But we don't worship Our Lady at our meetings. We don't put the Virgin on a pedestal. We invite her to take a seat among us. Gradually, we begin to hear her in one another's voices. In learning how to talk with one another, we learn how to talk to Our Lady—spontaneously, playfully, honestly.

The spiritual friends we need for a rosary circle are usually there for us from the start. Some may be family members. Others we will have known for years. After a while, people we haven't even met will hear that we pray the rosary and begin to seek us out. Our Lady wouldn't give us the beads without adding love to the mix. Not giving us rosary friends would be like giving us seeds and dirt, but no water or sunlight. Without spiritual friendships, how could we possibly grow?

Call Me Mother, Daughter, Sister, Lover, Bride.
But know that I am not limited to these roles.
I am Matchmaker and Midwife as well,
and the trusted Confidante you turn to in times of trouble.
Talk with Me at length in such circumstances,
as you would to your closest Girlfriend,
and I'm sure we can figure things out.

The Sacred Well of Mystery

MYSTERIES TAKE US ON A JOURNEY AWAY FROM DOGMA, not toward it. There is no single answer to a mystery, no fixed meaning. Mysteries are not puzzles to be solved, or even koans to be figured out—they are bottomless wells we can drink from again and again. They can revive us, sustain us, and even heal us if we let them.

With each decade of the rosary, we announce a new mystery and disappear inside of it with the prayers. We may visualize the scene, wonder about what it means, remember similar moments from our own lives or our own history as a species, simply daydream, or begin to question where we are headed. It's up to us. What we don't do is stay stuck in one place.

Mystery leads to mystery, round and round. In one moment we are with a young mother holding her baby in her arms; in another, we stand beside her at the foot of the cross. Sometimes we are the child lost at the Temple, at other times we are the mother anxiously concerned about the child who has disappeared.

As we pray the rosary, we reflect on each of these mysteries in turn. But how we do this is never prescribed. We follow Our Lady's lead, and our own imaginations, and trust that we will find our way. Compassion begins in imagination, in the ability to shift perspectives. Meditating on the mysteries puts the mind in a flexible, creative mode. It leaves us open to new thoughts and new ways of looking at the trials and triumphs of life.

Tellingly, it was the artists and not the priests who passed the mysteries along in the beginning. The first rosary manuals were picture books of wood-block illustrations that set the drama of the rosary directly before the eye. Things got into the rosary through art that religion would never have allowed: traces of the pagan and the erotic, for instance, and legends that everyone still believed, even though they couldn't be found in the Bible. These artists knew instinctively that the events they were depicting were not just historic moments but iconic representations of scenes that were always happening. At any moment the angel might appear and call forth the life from within each of us.

With the rosary, Our Lady tells a story that invites us to tell our story. Just as friends will sit down together and begin trading tales of babies being born, the woes of family members, and inexplicable experiences of the miraculous, the mysteries of the rosary encourage us to find the overlaps of our lives within these sacred rhythms. Each time we circle our beads we are finding a new story to tell. We are not locked into one symbolic narrative—we are freed into narrative possibility. There is no one story. A mystery doesn't tell us what to think; it changes the way we experience the reality of our world.

There are so many things in this world
that silence the voice and the heart.
It is a victory simply to share them.

What If I Don't Get It Right?

WHAT HAPPENS IF WE GET TOO BUSY AND FORGET TO say the rosary? Does that mean that we need to say an extra set of beads the following day? The rosary is a daily devotion, after all. We say the Joyful Mysteries one day, the Sorrowful the next, and the Glorious the day after that. Then we start over. But what if that kind of regularity seems beyond us?

Needless to say, the rosary shouldn't add to our burdens. Prayed in the right spirit, it should make life easier, not more complicated. As long as we are judging our efforts based on attention, attendance, performance, or piety, we are avoiding intimacy with Our Lady.

A surprising example of that kind of avoidance comes from the story of Juan Diego and Our Lady of Guadalupe. Juan is the archetypal "servant of Our Lady," responsive to her wishes and dedicated to fulfilling her requests as quickly and fully as possible. Except that he wasn't—although most people aren't familiar with that part of the story.

After twice failing to convince the bishop that he had seen the Virgin Mary, Juan returned to the hill at Tepeyac to confer with her again. She told him to come back the following day, promising at that time to give him the proof the bishop required. Only the next day Juan didn't show. He didn't forget to keep his appointment with the Virgin, *he decided not to go.*

That morning Juan's uncle had become seriously ill and Juan stayed home to care for him. By the early hours of December 12, the older man had taken a turn for the worse, and Juan set out for the village to fetch a priest to offer him last rites.

To get there he would have to pass by the very hill where the Virgin had appeared to him, so he took an alternate route in order to avoid her. It seems that Our Lady chose to appear not to an unquestioning follower of rules but to a very ordinary, very human individual uncertain about how to meet his many obligations. But instead of behaving in an angry or vengeful manner, she simply left the hilltop where she'd arranged to meet him and intercepted him along the way.

When Juan explained his absence, Our Lady of Guadalupe answered with words that are now famous throughout the world.

Do not be troubled or weighed down with grief.
Do not fear any illness or vexation, anxiety or pain.
Am I not here who am your Mother?

She gave Juan Diego a cloakful of flowers to take to the bishop, and when he returned to his uncle's house he discovered that, miraculously, the older man was completely healed.

So what happens when we miss an appointment with Our Lady? What happens when we're too distracted or worried or involved with other things and miss saying the rosary that day? What happens when we miss our rosary circle for weeks at a time?

Our Lady answers that question with one of her own: "Am I not here who am your Mother?" She follows us wherever we go.

Eventually we learn that the concerns of daily life are exactly the concerns of the rosary. They don't compete with each other. If anything, the rosary helps us with them. And, strange to say, those concerns help us with the rosary, because we often pray more earnestly in times of need. When we are anxious and worried, the rosary is the perfect place to turn.

There's no hurry. Our Lady is patient, and we're on nobody's schedule but our own.

When a child is learning to walk,
the mother doesn't particularly care
which direction the child goes in,
because learning to walk is the point.
Nevertheless, she will keep him
from stepping off a ledge.

No One Gets Left Out

According to one medieval legend, there are two gates of heaven. One is the front door, the other is at the back. The front gate is rigorously guarded and kept under lock and key. Only one key exists, and it belongs to Saint Peter—who, in medieval times, was a kind of stand-in for the pope. The other door was never locked, or even guarded, because Our Lady was in charge of it. If religions are made of rules that believers are expected to obey, the Virgin is ready to bend them. That seems to be her job.

Once there was a sacristan at the Church of St. Peter in Rome who had a special devotion to Our Lady. It happened that one day the lamp before her shrine began to grow dim and was on the verge of burning out. Being old and somewhat lazy, he decided to remedy the situation by taking some oil from the lamp that burned in honor of Saint Peter, thinking that surely Peter would not begrudge a little oil to give to God's Mother what she needed. But the saint was profoundly vexed at this. Peter believed that, in his own church at least, he stood above all the other saints, including the Queen of Angels.

That night he descended from paradise and appeared to the poor sacristan as he slept.

"Why have you taken oil from my lamp!" Peter demanded.

"I only borrowed a little, that Our Lady's lamp might be fed," the sacristan replied.

"God's Mother is honored in many lands," declared the wrathful saint, "and many shrines and pilgrimages are established in her name. But this is my house, in which *my* body lies, the very Rock upon which the Church was built, and I will not suffer you to honor the Lady Mary above me in this way."

Peter then added that, as the keeper of the keys of heaven, he had the prerogative to deny entry to whomsoever he chose. "Because you have given me less oil than the Virgin, I shall surely shut the door in your face."

The sacristan awoke full of dread and foreboding and hurried to the church to refill the oil in Peter's lamp, yet with little hope, for he knew the saint to be a hasty and a vengeful man. That very night, however, the Virgin herself appeared to console him as he slept.

"Fear not, and continue to honor me as you have done before. For although the Apostle Peter keeps the keys to the gate of heaven, I am the keeper of its window. For the door of heaven is very narrow, and Peter guards it strictly, but the window of my love is very wide."

It comes as a shock to modern people to see Peter, the first pope, portrayed as a villain. But Christians of earlier centuries were used to this kind of story. The tale was part of an oral tradition kept alive as an antidote to the punishments and prohibitions of the Church.

Such tales (and there were many of them) told the story of a Mother who wasn't overly scrupulous when it came to human weakness. She wasn't a gatekeeper or a policeman, like Peter. She was a window left open to anyone who needed to climb through—so no one would ever be locked out.

Today we can still enter that open portal by praying the rosary. Efforts are continuously being made by the Church to regulate or restrict its use, but such efforts are destined to always fail. No one can close the portal of the rosary. The only person that Peter can turn away from heaven is the one who thinks the front door is the only gate there is.

Set the dark clouds at your back
and step forward into the light.
Take my hand and I will lead you.
I am very good at watching people's backs.

Pass It On

FELLOWSHIPS CALLED "CONFRATERNITIES" HELPED SPREAD the rosary incredibly fast during the Middle Ages. It cost nothing to become a member and anyone could join. Most members were illiterate. What they needed to know to pray the rosary they learned orally when somebody taught them the prayers—or visually from pamphlets illustrating the mysteries. That was all they had to know.

The truth is, the rosary spread itself. It was so innately comforting and satisfying, it didn't need to be advertised. It showed a knack for finding its way into people's lives.

The only requirement for membership in a confraternity was a desire to pray the rosary. Because they charged no dues, the confraternities were open to the poor. Remarkably for that era, they welcomed women as well. Their members weren't penalized for not saying the rosary if the demands of daily living got in the way. Nor were they required to make up the days they missed (unless they wanted to) by praying extra rosaries. In the beginning, confraternity members weren't even required to pray the *same* rosary. There were a variety of methods. Members adapted the rosary to meet their individual needs.

Medieval rosary confraternities offered the "spiritual but not religious" alternative of their day. Perhaps the closest equivalent we have now is AA, which likewise accepts all members, charges no dues for membership, and takes a vigorous hands-off approach to overseeing the activities of its various groups.

When it comes to creating fellowship, nothing could be more practical from a spiritual point of view. The rosary is a string of beads, true—but there are no strings attached. It is ours to do with as we please. We can take what we need from it, when we need it, and use it in the way that feels best for our lives. Our Lady teaches us to listen to our hearts and trust them.

When a bunch of people meet in a room to pray together, the rosary helps create a healthy spiritual community. If a group gets so big that it no longer feels cozy, it solves the problem in the same way that AA groups have learned to solve it. Another group tends to form naturally. That is how fellowships grow.

Near the end of *Not-God*, his history of Alcoholics Anonymous, Ernest Kurtz traced the rapid spread of the movement back to a single factor: *one alcoholic talking to another*. What people had lost by the early twentieth century—what they craved and what they needed, not just to maintain their sobriety but to find the happiness that had eluded them in the first place—was fellowship. That, according to Kurtz, was what made Alcoholics Anonymous work so well that it became the template for dozens of other 12-step groups: its emphasis on strong horizontal relationships between members of equal status.

We don't need hierarchy to create a spiritual movement, it turns out. And we certainly don't need lots of rules. We don't even need a church. All we need is a rosary, a room to meet in or a tree to sit under, and a group of spiritual friends.

To pray for your heart's desire and receive your heart's desire
is to be a great valley through which a river flows,

bringing flowers to the fields on either side of
its path as it goes.
Pass this on. Give it to others.
Know that, as I give you graces in answer to your prayers,
these graces will be too big for you to hold.
You must give them to others.
They are not for you alone.

The Human Agenda

ALTHOUGH THEY WOULD NEVER SEE THEMSELVES AS SIMILAR, the fundamentalist and the scientific atheist have more in common than they think. Both view human beings as the pinnacle of creation. One believes that humans are made in the image of God, the other that humans basically *are* gods, capable of understanding the workings of the universe and entitled to do with it whatever they please.

In our infatuation with the fruits of modern industry and technology, we tend to forget that science and religion arose together roughly twelve thousand years ago, just following the last Ice Age. The first sciences were astronomy and agriculture, which, working in tandem, allowed us to predict yearly changes in climate and begin to manipulate our environment to control our food supply. Gradually, we changed our relationships with plants and animals, becoming their masters, and experimented with ways of increasing our flocks and fields. Eventually we created rationales for the new way of life we had adopted for ourselves and imposed upon our fellow creatures—and in this way religion was born.

Throughout history, each new set of "improvements" to the human condition has brought with it all kinds of unexpected problems that then had to be solved with further "improvements." Vast fields of a single crop seemed like a solution to the problems of a fickle food supply—until the locusts descended or the rains stopped falling or the soil became so depleted that it had to be enriched with fertilizers and poisoned with pesticides in order to yield as it had before. Monoculture leads to monotheism . . . leads to Monsanto. It is hard to imagine, in retrospect, how this could have gone anywhere but wrong.

In the middle of the rosary, in the inexorable swiftness of a single twenty-four hours, Jesus is arrested, tortured, and executed. This is neither a natural death nor an inevitable process. Nevertheless, it is an effective symbolic summary for what we have done to the natural world, to our fellow creatures, and ultimately to ourselves. In the name of justice, righteousness, and progress we commit murder. The real fruit of Our Lady's womb is life on Earth, and for a long time now we have been nailing it to the cross.

Praying the rosary brings us face to face with the heartbreak of all we have done in the name of civilization. But it doesn't leave us there. Coming to terms with the sorrows of the human agenda is the only way we can move beyond them. For the rosary also reminds us that life is mysteriously resilient. After the flood, there is fertile ground where before there was only sand. After the fire, seeds hidden deep in the earth crack open, sprout, and bloom.

People think that humans have ordered the world,
but when I look at "human order," I see chaos.
So many of your anxieties come from the fear
of chaos and disorder,
but in reality you are the chaos and disorder.
It would be laughable if it didn't cause so much sadness.

Our Lady of the Beasts

As civilization developed, so grew the belief that animals were dumb beasts, incapable of language, intelligence, or emotion. We are not animals, we tell ourselves, so why should we listen to them? Yet the oldest stories from around the world recognize all kinds of creatures as messengers, helpers, and even divinities. For a people still in conversation with nature, every animal had something to say. Birds bore messages from the dead, spiders wove stories, and coyotes lurked in the shadows to remind us that we were not quite as clever as we thought.

Some of the earliest statues of the Goddess portray her with the wings of a vulture, the feet of a bird, or the head of a hippo. Even when she is depicted as fully human, she is rarely without her animal companions—the great cats who stride beside her, the owls who perch on her shoulder, the peacocks whose feathers, covered in eyes, are so like her many hands. Often her children are animals as well—part hawk or part goat or part elephant. One of the earliest known names of the Goddess, apart from Mother of All Life, was Our Lady of the Beasts.

In the Nativity, Mary gives birth in a stable and lays her newborn child in a *manger*—a feed trough for animals. The Gospel writer makes no mention of any beasts at the birth of Jesus, but artists always include them. That Jesus is born amid the animals, as *food* for the animals, is part of the message of the story.

All beings in the natural world are interdependent. The death of one becomes life for another. A mouse dies and the owl eats. The corpse of a deer nourishes the flies that will feed the birds. Even the seeming waste of excrement feeds the soil and spreads seeds. Our own bodies, even while we are alive, support microbes and bacteria, which in turn regulate our immune systems and our moods. A tree falls and from its rotted bark grow fungi and flowers. "Take, eat—this is my body," Jesus will say to his disciples, holding up the bread on the night before his crucifixion. It isn't a metaphor. The world is all one body—in which we eat . . . and are eaten. By denying that we are animals, we are expressing our desire to transcend this fundamental reality of ecology.

In refusing to acknowledge the nonhuman voices all around us, we have cut ourselves off, not just from the creatures who are our guides and our friends, but from those sources of wisdom within ourselves that come from our animal nature. We have reduced the mystery of consciousness to mere thinking, privileging logic and reason over dreams and visions and intuitions. We have turned the world into a machine that, with a little tinkering, we might finally manage to get just right. In truth, the belief in our singularity and supremacy has left us vulnerable and alone.

Were we to listen to them, even now the animals would tell us what we have forgotten: That we're all in this together. That we drink the same water, breathe the same air, and live—at present—within a narrow range of temperatures conducive to our survival. The animals would tell us to spend less time looking at ourselves, thinking about ourselves, talking about ourselves, and more time looking around us at the world that gave us our bodies and sustains our lives from one generation to the next.

Any real solution to the cascading problems that face humanity in the coming century will not be a further step away from the natural world into some bright and shining technological future.

What will save us is the wisdom the animals have never forgotten—that our comings and goings from this world are eternal and that nothing dies but something is reborn.

Basic sanity is knowing that there is no difference
between humans and animals.
If you understood this,
you wouldn't have any other questions
about the world.

A Bull Given to Saint Mary

MANY OF THE STORIES IN *THE MIRACLES OF OUR LADY OF Rocamadour* contain teachings that were most likely hidden from the pious authorities of their day. This is certainly true in the tale about a lost bull. In that story, a man who owned many cattle promised his best bull to the Lady in order to gain her blessing. But no sooner had he done so than an enemy stole his entire herd. Now, in addition to having lost his livelihood, he had no way to honor his vow to the Virgin.

And yet, as he cried and prayed, something wondrous occurred. The very bull he had promised to Our Lady, which the man was certain was just an animal without any sense, escaped from the enemy's enclosure. As if it knew exactly what it was doing, the bull knocked the bolt from the fence and led all the stolen animals back to their owner's door.

Overjoyed at his good fortune, the man journeyed to Rocamadour. "And when he came to the doors of the church of the blessed and glorious Virgin," wrote the scribe, "it was not the man who led the bull, but rather the bull who led the man—like a guide who knew the way, never deviating from the path to the left or right."

The people of twelfth-century France would have connected the animal in the story with the bullfights common in that region. Another, even older part of their consciousness, however, would have associated bulls with the power of the returning life force in the spring. Tens of thousands of years before this story was recorded, people living in that same area of the world identified that life force with the constellation Taurus. A paleoanthropologist recently discovered a diagram of that very constellation in Lascaux Cave—superimposed over a painting of a bull.

In promising a bull, the man in the story is entrusting his hopes for future prosperity to Our Lady's hands. But the first thing that happens to him after he makes that vow is that he loses everything he has. It is interesting to note that his grief at this loss is spiritual rather than financial. But the reversal of fortune that follows is not exactly what it seems.

The story makes a point of the irrationality and insensibility of the bull, which acts "as if" it were capable of reason or volition. It would be easy to dismiss this part of the story as a standard Judeo-Christian trope on the inferiority of the animal nature, but the point of the story seems to suggest just the opposite. The bull remembers what human beings have forgotten. He remembers the Way of the Goddess, which is also the Way of the Seasons. The man in the story, wisely, becomes his follower in the end.

Even now, you persist in seeing yourself
as all-powerful, exceptional, and alone.
You are therefore without friends other than your kind.
If you asked them, the animals
would show you the way.
If you followed them,
the trees and grasses would take you home.

The Dead Are Right Here

WHILE TRADITIONAL ROSARIES HAVE FIVE DECADES, SOME occasionally had six. These can still be found in areas of Europe where the words *rose garden* once referred to an ancestral graveyard. These extra beads were used, after a set of mysteries had been completed, in order to pray for the dead.

Indigenous peoples around the world have long venerated their ancestors. The addition of specific beads to the rosary for remembering the departed was therefore understandable for recently Christianized people who wanted to maintain contact with the spirits of their loved ones. The Church eventually commodified this folk practice and assigned a numerical value to the prayers, whereby every rosary said lessened the time, by days and years, that a departed soul might have to spend in purgatory. But originally, as they are the world over, such prayers were a way of recognizing the continued presence of the dead in the lives of the living.

Before the modern era, the dead were always close. People usually died at home, where their loved ones washed and wrapped their bodies, becoming familiar with the heaviness of cold limbs that no longer coursed with blood. They were buried nearby where it was easy to visit them and think about their bones. All kinds of lore reminded people how to commune with the souls of those who had passed on. The rosary was recognized as a portal to the land of the dead—not just a way of remembering those who were gone, but a means of communicating with them as well. Even today, psychics and mediums are often devoted to the rosary for just that purpose.

Not only have we lost our intimacy with death in the modern world but we have lost our conversation with the dead—and we have lost their wisdom, too. For if the dead need our prayers for healing, we are in need of their guidance as well.

Below us and behind us are legions of the dead. We trace our ancestries back to distant countries and religions and migrations—to cousins we cannot imagine, mothers whose names are forgotten, and peoples whose languages and lands are forever gone. If we keep going, our ancestral lines merge eventually with vanished hominids, with tiny mammals, and somewhere, billions of years ago, with cells beginning to divide in the primordial seas. Given a chance, what would the dead tell us about where we have come from, where we are now, and where we are going next?

We can slip our rosaries under our pillows or wrap them around our wrists when we sleep so that we can commune in our dreams with those who have come before us. We can place rosaries in the hands of the dying and recite the names of our loved ones on our beads. But most of all, whenever we pray the rosary, we can remember that the dead hear us, love us, and are ready to offer to us their wisdom. For it is the dead who know, at last, what life is really for.

The dead wish nothing more
than to reassure the living.
The dead are always disappointed and surprised
when people look away from them.

They are blossoms, the dead.
What looks like a dead body
on this side of the veil
is a flower on the other.

A Sword in Our Hearts

Life leads us through sorrow. There is no getting away from that truth in the rosary. Whatever miracles and resurrections are to come lie on the other side of the tomb. Before a seed can grow, it must fall to the ground and lie dormant and trusting in the darkness of the soil. Eventually, when the conditions are right, it will break open, and out of that brokenness a plant will begin to grow. Out of that brokenness, all things grow. Life devours itself, and life feeds itself. Everything returns to the dirt, and everything emerges from the dirt—from the lowest lichens to the greatest civilizations. There are no exceptions. No truth could be more fundamental than this.

In modern life we often reel from one televised outrage to another—while averting our eyes from the everyday miseries all around us. We warehouse the elderly, quarantine the sick, and rarely view the bodies of our dead. Drained of blood, our meat arrives wrapped in plastic at the grocery store. Whole forests have vanished for the fields that grow our soybeans and our corn. There are wastelands of garbage the size of countries floating in our oceans and toxic dumps a few miles from every city, large or small. How do we look at what we have done (and are still doing) without turning away—or collapsing in despair?

To cope with that much sorrow, some of us try to winnow it down by fixating on a particular issue. If only we outlawed guns, abortion, factory farming, or fill in your cause—then, perhaps, the sufferings of the world would become more manageable. Others among us simply refuse to admit how dire things have become. We cover our ears when ecologists tell us that we have passed the tipping point for mass extinction. When our scientists warn that rising temperatures will create billions of climate refugees by century's end, we resolutely look away.

The rosary can help us to remain present and openhearted in the face of such sorrow. What we are teaching ourselves is that we can move through it, bead by bead, prayer by prayer, until we reach the mysteries of rebirth. The rosary does not promise us some blissed-out enlightenment that will help us transcend suffering and sorrow forever. Instead, it shows us, with Our Lady's help, how we can come through them—with greater wisdom and understanding, and true empathy for the sufferings of others in our world.

On the day of his death, as Jesus carries his cross, Mary bears witness to the inexorable march of pain. She doesn't betray him like Judas, deny him like Peter, or abandon him like the other disciples. But she also can't stop it. She follows him to the execution ground and remains close as he suffers.

Our Lady of Sorrows was a well-known title for Mary during the Middle Ages, honoring the Mother who could listen to the cries of the world without covering her ears, the Lady who could bear witness to its sadness without looking away.

The Sorrowful Mother usually wore black. Sometimes she held her slain son on her lap. Always her gaze was direct and unflinching. In most versions she stared directly at the viewer, pulling her robe apart with one hand to reveal a heart pierced through with a sword. This is not the compliant, primly poised sorrow of religious piety. This is *powerful* sorrow. This is the sorrow of the goddess Tiamat in the *Enuma Elish* with Marduk's arrow still lodged within her—a sorrow that goes so far down, and so far back in time, it touches the bottom of human history.

Without a willingness to pass through suffering, there is no way to acknowledge our own struggles and failures, our losses and temporary defeats—and no way of cultivating compassion for others.

There is a time for keening and a place for sorrow. That is what we learn from the rosary. Just as the world must pass through winter to get to spring, we must pray the Sorrowful Mysteries to get to the Glorious Mysteries, where joy is restored, wisdom is won, and the divine union of male and female energies, now reconciled and balanced, can renew and regreen the Earth. But there is no way to reach that resurrection without passing through the darkness and desolation of the tomb.

The heart is the only place where people
can still feel My tears.
Their ears can no longer hear My weeping,
their heads are endlessly busy.
But the heart is still sometimes sensitive enough
to feel the burn of a tear.

PART IV

THIS VALLEY OF TEARS

The Boy Drawer

NOT LONG AFTER OUR LADY WOKE ME IN THE MIDDLE OF the night with her strange promise about a "column of saints" that would support my prayer, friends began asking me to teach them the rosary. I was so caught off guard by these requests in the beginning that I often simply gave them the rosary I was using and told them to keep it, explaining the basic prayers. I lost a lot of rosaries that way. No sooner would I purchase another at the flea market than I'd find myself handing it over, sometimes to a perfect stranger. Sometimes this happened *at* the flea market, before I could even get it home. Eventually I learned to carry an extra rosary in my pocket.

Although it pleased me, I did not know what to think about any of this. Beginning that night on Cape Cod, I said the rosary faithfully, though not always perfectly, and I read a great deal about its history and practice. But, somehow, I still didn't feel entitled to it. It wasn't as if the rosary had been passed down to me in my family. I couldn't help but feel like a bit of an impostor sometimes when I began to recite my prayers. At times I felt

I had *stolen* the rosary. I couldn't shake off the feeling that the rosary might be something I couldn't have as a non-Catholic, or shouldn't be allowed to have.

But something happened the following spring that changed all that for me.

My grandmother's house in Forrest City, Arkansas, was being sold to pay for her care since, at 102, she could no longer live on her own and needed to move to a nursing home. My mother had called the week before to ask if there was anything I wanted from the house I had lived in as a young boy. If so, I had better come and claim it now. I was debating whether to make the trip or not when I had the following dream.

I am with my mother in Forrest City, visiting my grandmother's house one last time. But as soon as I walk in, instead of looking through its many rooms and cupboards and closets, I go right to the kitchen, to the "boy drawer."

As the child of a single mother, I had been cared for when I was little by the woman who had also raised my mother, my uncle, and my aunt. To entertain me, Josephine kept a drawer full of tops and jacks and Slinkys—toys we bought on our weekly walk into town to shop at the Benjamin Franklin five-and-dime store. She called it the "boy drawer" because it was where she had kept my uncle's toys when he was small.

When I open the boy drawer in my dream, however, instead of the toys of my childhood, the first thing I see is a beautiful onyx and sterling Catholic rosary. "This is all I need," I say to my mother, taking the rosary in hand and placing it in my pocket. "This was what I came for. It's all right now if you want to sell the house."

I awoke feeling strangely moved by this dream, which I shared with my youngest sister, Elizabeth. I never did enter the house again in reality, having made my peace with its loss in my sleep.

But that was not the end of it.

A few weeks later, I was shopping for an antique rosary on eBay, one I hoped to keep in the family and pass down to my son, Jonah, who, having been taught the rosary by Perdita when he was little, would never doubt that it belonged to him. After much searching, I found a beautiful old set of beads with double-lock chain links made in the 1950s by the Creed Rosary Company.

Legendary for their craftsmanship, these "unbreakable" rosaries were highly prized by collectors and therefore prohibitively expensive. But this rosary was modestly priced. In her description, the vendor explained that there was some pitting in the silver of the crucifix and the center medallion, but that the rosary was otherwise sound. Well, at least it was well used, I remember thinking, and maybe an heirloom. The pitting probably just added to its charm.

I purchased the rosary and was notified by email the following day that my package had departed from the post office in Wynne, Arkansas.

It is difficult to describe the effect the name of that town had on me. My grandmother and great-grandmother, along with my great-aunts and great-uncles, had all been born and raised in Wynne, a mere quarter hour's drive from Forrest City. If my family had anything like an ancestral burial ground, it was the dirt of that tiny delta town.

Filled with an uncanny sense of anticipation, I contacted the seller and discovered that her name was Rose France, formerly Rose Clark of Forrest City, where she had also been born and raised.

It turned out that Rose's father had been my grandmother's mechanic, and that Rose herself had worked as the "toy and cotton candy girl" at Ben Franklin's as a teenager. I asked how old she was, but I needn't have bothered. Still in that déjà vu–like place, I knew the answer already. She was the girl who had sold me the toys for the boy drawer on my weekly trips to town with Josephine.

It was Elizabeth who made the connection when I called to tell her about all of this. "Just like in your dream," she said.

The next day, when I went out to the mailbox to retrieve the package, I saw from Rose's return address that she lived on Ellis Street. My grandmother had been an Ellis, and when I later mentioned this to Rose, she told me that she was descended from James Ellis—which meant that we were, in fact, related. Things like this happened so often after Our Lady appeared that Perdita and I would just laugh when they did. But this was still early on.

That was the last time I worried about whether or not I was entitled to pray the rosary as a non-Catholic.

Needless to say, the dream stayed with me. And every time I prayed with those silver and onyx beads, I thought about the boy drawer. Eventually that led to a question.

Had there ever been a "girl drawer," where the female members of the family kept their toys?

I asked Elizabeth, but she just laughed, screwing up her face in an expression of mock incredulity. "Duh . . . *No!* Of course there was no girl drawer."

I asked my mother, my aunt, my other sister, and my female cousins, and the answer was the same. The older women said, "No. Why do you ask?" The younger expressed varying degrees of irritation that it was only now, when it no longer mattered, that I was asking a question I should have known the answer to all along.

But I didn't know the answer. I hadn't even known to ask the question. I had never thought of it before.

And that, I realized, was how I ended up in Zen.

The Buddhism I embraced in my twenties was the ultimate boy drawer, filled with lots of toys especially designed for men. Like the priestly communities of other religions, it involved plenty of rules to follow and rituals to master. Conformity trumped creativity, obedience was better than originality, and acquiescence to authority was the most highly prized virtue of all.

You could be shunned or even ousted from that community for questioning the pronouncements of those above you; your place in the pecking order was rigorously defined. That order was hierarchical, ascending through levels of mastery, each with its own secret handshake and set of privileges conferred by the tradition. And that tradition, having endured for thousands of years, was by definition more important than the needs of any individual. The desires of the heart had no place in it . . . unless, of course, your desire was to rise to the top of the heap. In that case, there was a well-worn path to success: Keep your head down, don't poke your nose where it doesn't belong, and do (and believe) as you are told.

From the age of nineteen until I left Zen, at thirty-three, I lived, breathed, and excelled in that world. Only I didn't. Not really. There is always the illusion of winning at the boy game. If that is all you know because it is all you have been taught, or if you're callous and don't care about anything but success in ascending those vertical hierarchies, then maybe the illusion is enough. It was not enough for me.

By 1990 I was on the verge of becoming a Zen master in my own right, with the goal of adding my name to an all-star, all-boy lineage that traced its authority clear back to the Buddha. Until I started waking up each morning so depressed I couldn't get out of bed.

Had I known then what I know now, I would have been angry instead. Possibly, I would have intervened and tried to change the abusive religious culture that had consumed all the energy and enthusiasm of my youth. But doing that would have meant becoming brokenhearted and broken open, and I wasn't ready for that yet. So I left. Two years later I met Perdita, and a year after that I took a job as senior editor of *Tricycle: The Buddhist Review*.

It was easier to look at Buddhism, and really see it, once I was no longer affiliated with any one sect or school. And I saw *a lot* of it—too much to continue in the naïve belief that it was a more enlightened form of religion. There were the predictable scandals about sex and money, which are always a problem, simply because they are endemic to religion itself. There were all the subtler forms of extortion, too, often disguised as fundraising campaigns. And then there were the casualties, endless casualties, of lives that put religious ideals ahead of personal happiness, sometimes even personal safety. The members took care of the religion. But nobody looked after them.

One day years later, after I'd begun praying the rosary again, I received a call from a *New York Times* reporter asking if the allegations of sexual misconduct against the Japanese abbot of the monastery where I had trained were true. I'd been expecting something like this for twenty years and wasn't surprised when he told me that I was the first person he had called.

I told him everything I knew. But later I was haunted by the one thing I hadn't told him: that I had chosen to focus on my own spiritual ambitions during those years rather than notice the many abuses of power that were happening right under my nose. I chose not to notice the abbot's seductions of female students, his intimidation of them after these relationships inevitably ended, and the many ways he spiritually destabilized everyone in the community with these affairs. I hadn't allowed myself to see any of this because I hadn't *wanted* to see it. Which made it ridiculously easy for the abbot to continue in this pattern. It wasn't just that the patriarchal obsession with building and maintaining a religious empire was inherently dangerous, leaving countless victims in its wake. In colluding with its agenda, I had become dangerous, too.

The abbot was eventually forced to resign, and sometime later I received an invitation to attend a "reconciliation gathering" in Manhattan. The former abbot himself had called for the meeting, ostensibly to take responsibility for his behavior as a sexual predator over a period of almost fifty years. I was pretty sure it was pointless to go, but I went anyway. Given my culpability in all that had happened, it was a penance I couldn't refuse.

Of course, the venue for the event was all wrong. A Unitarian chapel hardly seemed like a sinister choice, but I understood at once why the Zen master had chosen it. Even the Unitarians couldn't escape the tilted playing field of authoritarian religion. The seating was all in pews.

There the master was, positioned at the front of the room, and we had no choice but to face the front. That privileged position was what he knew . . . and it was what we knew as well. I felt a cord of panic draw tight within me. The room suddenly felt too close and small. I looked around me, pretty sure that everyone else must be feeling it, too. But it was hard to tell. I could only see their backs.

Why didn't we all just get up and leave? At the very least, why didn't we insist that he reposition his chair in the middle of the chapel so that those in the front pews would have to turn around? I don't like the answer I have come up with, but I am certain it's the truth. It was easier to submit to authority that one last time than turn to face the heartbreak in one another's faces.

The fourth person to speak was a woman in her early thirties. With impressive dignity and self-possession, she made her case in a way that left little wiggle room for the master. She told him how confused and emotionally devastated she had become as the result of his actions. They had made her question her vocation and fractured her sense of self. Did he understand how much long-term trauma he had caused, not only to her but to every member of the community—especially its women? Could he appreciate how spiritually desolate she had felt?

The event facilitator, a woman trained in conflict resolution, asked the abbot if he could mirror back to this woman what she had said to him in order to demonstrate that he had understood her.

"Ah . . ." he replied, stalling for a moment to formulate his response. He then spoke slowly, enunciating the words in his best, most studied English: "I understand that she was confused in her Zen practice."

There was a collective gasp. It was as though he had sucked all the air out of the room.

This was why we had come? *This* was what he had understood?

A gray-haired woman stood up suddenly, visibly weeping, and scooted out of her pew, bumping quickly past people's knees. "There's just so much violence in the world . . . so much violence in the world," she muttered as she left. I followed her out the door.

I walked down Madison Avenue, passing some of the most expensive boutiques and specialty stores on Earth. One, Velsani Antiques, was selling a life-size medieval statue of Our Lady of Sorrows for roughly the price of our Woodstock home. On almost every street corner, for two dozen blocks, was a homeless veteran. I couldn't imagine the horrors they must have seen. I wondered where their mothers were, and what kind of sorrow they must have been feeling that night.

I knew I needed to get someplace else as fast as I could. The problem was, where did you go to escape from the evils of empire when empire was all you knew? Given the accusations of sexual abuse against thousands of Catholic priests around the world, St. Patrick's Cathedral was hardly a logical choice. In our rosary circle were survivors who, decades later, were only just beginning to find the courage to tell their stories. How did you even reform such institutions when they were built on the oppression of women and children from the get-go?

Out of the frying pan and into the fire, I thought as the familiar spires of the cathedral rose up adjacent to Rockefeller Center. Then I remembered that there was a chapel dedicated to Our Lady at the very back of the apse.

There were pews in this chapel, too, but it didn't matter. It was completely empty. So I knelt up front at the rail before the statue of the Virgin. With her hands held upright, palms open, she looked like she was about to catch a ball, or maybe the planet. I prayed the latter was true.

The bus ride back to Woodstock found me too desolate even to pray. It was dark outside as we neared that area of New Jersey called the Meadowlands, where mobsters once dumped the bodies of their victims. The chemical toxicity of that blasted wasteland seemed like a fitting conclusion to the day.

Finally, I said to Our Lady: "I have no idea what to do with this terrible mess you've caused me to see. Maybe climate change is a mercy, given what the world has come to. Tell me what to do. Give me a sign. I couldn't be more lost."

I looked out the window of the bus at that precise moment and saw a giant, brilliantly lit billboard with a profile of the Virgin Mary. It bore only three words in four-foot-high block letters. PRAY THE ROSARY! it said.

Well, I thought, I did ask for a sign.

It was what she always said in such circumstances anyway. Whether she was talking to a middle-aged ex-Buddhist or a peasant girl in Portugal, her core advice was always the same. So I did as she asked and prayed the rosary in the dark all the way back to Woodstock.

A few months later, Our Lady told us to take a trip to Cape Cod so that Perdita could gather "the dirt of your ancestors." A bit of soil from whatever graves Perdita could find would be enough. The dead all knew one another, so there was no reason to feel anxious. If she missed anyone, the others would bring them along.

We drove to Centerville, where, scraping a bit of soil into her tin from the grave of another Finn we'd found, Perdita looked up over her shoulder and said, "You know, you're gonna need to do this too at some point, right?"

I said yes, I'd thought of that. But I wasn't sure how soon that would happen. Five minutes later I got the call from my mother telling me that my grandmother had just died.

I arrived in Arkansas without a tin like Perdita's for collecting the dirt of my ancestors. I'd packed quickly and hadn't even remembered to bring a necktie. But when I explained to my mother what was needed, she drove to an antiques emporium that was basically an indoor flea market and bought one for me herself.

At the cemetery, after the burial, everyone volunteered to help, and we found as many graves as we could. Strangely, no one seemed surprised by this request. Dirt was a thing in that part of Arkansas. Ask anyone in Forrest City what it was known for before the Walmart moved in and everything got paved over, and they'd tell you that it was the jewel on the buckle of the "Black Belt," so called because of its rich, dark Mississippi delta soil.

You could dig down a dozen feet in my grandmother's backyard without ever hitting a single stone. I know this because as a boy I tried it more than once. I grew up with that dirt between my toes and never once thought of it as "dirty." It was too rich and wonderful for that. And aromatic, too. My earliest memories are all saturated with its smell.

Especially after a rainfall, you could step outside and the smell of dirt was as big as Arkansas. It gave you the feeling that if you stood still long enough in one place, your toes would put down roots and flowers would pop out of your eyes. I used to find arrowheads in that dirt when I was a boy—prizes I treasured and kept in their own special box inside the boy drawer. But it was only half a century later that I understood their significance.

I was reading a book on the black Egyptian goddess Isis, whom Plutarch identified with the soil of the Nile delta, when I was struck by a peculiar irony—the area around Memphis, Tennessee, just to the east of Forrest City, had been continuously inhabited by human beings for roughly twice as long as Memphis, Egypt, the capital of the Old Kingdom, from which it had derived its name. It was one of those historic details that reshuffles your brain, putting an entirely new set of cards on top. The arrowheads I'd picked out of the dirt as a child had belonged to a people who had lived there for ten thousand years before me. My grandfather had made his living farming that dark soil, but he was a newcomer where the land was concerned. The evidence of it was there below him, being turned up constantly by his plow.

The people in Forrest City used to say of a very old person that he or she was "older than dirt." I remember wondering in my literal, childlike way how old dirt was and what, if anything, was older. The answer came in another, similar expression I sometimes heard: "Older than God's Mother." Being good Protestant folk, they weren't talking about the Virgin Mary, or not the conventional Virgin in any case. The people of that town sensed they were living atop a loam-like column of saints that stretched down clear to the bottom of time. You couldn't live there without knowing that. The knowledge of it got into you through your nostrils and under your fingernails. It entered your dreams. It was part of everything you ate.

Late that night, in my motel room on the outskirts of town, I was restless and unable to sleep. It felt like there was a ghost convention going on inside my brain. Finally, I took my tin full of noisy ancestors and drove to the house I had lived in as a boy. The windows were dark. I wasn't sure if anyone was living there now. Regardless, to me it felt empty. My grandmother was gone. Josephine was gone. The house held nothing now but their spirits.

But the boy drawer was still there. I could feel it. I pulled the rosary from my pocket and said a decade of Hail Marys out there alone on the sidewalk in the dark.

It was one of those things that you can't explain and that therefore haunts you long after it has happened. The boy drawer had excluded the girls in my family in a way that should have seemed trivial after all this time but didn't, because it was an analog for so many other exclusions—a symbol for everything that had gone wrong. And yet, wasn't it in that very drawer that I had found the rosary in my dream? I had the feeling I was looking at something momentous, with far-reaching significance for my life. I just couldn't figure out what it was.

Finally I knelt down and, reaching my arm as far as I could through the fence, brought back a fistful of grass, brushing as much soil as I could get from the roots into my ancestor tin.

It was only when I was back at the motel and lying in bed that the obvious answer came to me. In that strange way dreams have of reflecting your life back to you in the form of a riddle, the solution had been there all along. I hadn't rescued the rosary from the boy drawer—it had rescued me.

I'd felt such spiritual longing all my life, restlessly moving from one path to another in my search for heaven or nirvana. With each new venture, I would summon the hope that *this* time I would find it: some enlightened, transcendent state that would take me above or beyond the mere matter of this world. That search ended the night My Girl woke me to pray the rosary. I was done with the boy drawer of religion. After that, I was never tempted by the sky. My place was with the dirt of this planet. And whenever I prayed the rosary, I knew that I was home.

Faster Than the Speed of Life

Coming to the rosary as a modern person can be a little like breaking down on a busy highway traveled by many people, all of them going too fast. In their daily quest for success, most travelers have forgotten that there are lakes and forests, fields and mountains—a whole world of things that have nothing to do with commuting or commerce—just on either side. With their attentions riveted by the white dividing line, the road is all they see.

Break down on a road like that and you are apt to experience disorientation, possibly even panic. Going at the same speed as everyone else can have a strangely steadying effect—even if you are deluded about where you are going or why you are going there . . . even if you are traveling much too fast.

Being stuck on the shoulder with hazard lights flashing is the archetypal modern emergency. Cars whiz by only a few feet away, buffeting your vehicle in their drafts. It's best at that point just to call for a lift or a tow truck. It would be dangerous to get out of the car, wouldn't it?

Nearly every book on modern Marian apparitions begins with Our Lady of the Miraculous Medal in 1830. And yet, not one of those books asks the obvious question: Why 1830? Why, beginning that year, did the Virgin Mary appear five hundred times in just under two centuries? What happened in 1830 that made her say to the Parisian nun Catherine Labouré, and to so many others she subsequently spoke to, "Evil times are coming . . . the entire world will be in distress"?

If you search the history books and time lines for some great event, you won't find it. There are the usual disasters and regime changes, but nothing that would account for a major global shift. Not unless you read old newspapers to see what people in Europe and America were most excited about that year. Then it makes a disturbing kind of sense.

Historians do not agree about the origins of our global economy, exactly when and where it began. But there is a case to be made that it started in 1830 with the creation of the first working railroads. Before rail transport, people traveled as fast as their feet could carry them, their horses could bear them, or the winds could drive their sails. Life was local; industry and agriculture were determined mostly by what resources lay nearby. Afterward, there seemed no limit to how fast human beings would go in the name of progress, or how far they would spread their influence around the globe.

Once our bodies began moving faster than our souls, there was no logic for retaining even our most rudimentary connection with the Earth. The ground was no longer our Mother but a source of friction that slowed us down. Increasingly, we strove to avoid her or rise above her or, at the very least, to minimize contact with her, speeding along on railways, roads, and highways—and, ultimately, through the air. There was no way even to pause and take stock of our lives, no way to stop and ask ourselves if this was truly what we wanted.

It isn't just that we are effectively now going faster than the speed of life. We no longer know what our lives are for. This is where we find ourselves today. Our speed of travel, speed of transaction, speed of communication, speed of technological innovation—these are supposed to enhance the quality of our lives. But our true quality of life is determined by our connection with our Mother.

The rosary offers a path that leads away from the frenetic, ongoing state of emergency of contemporary life. The beads aren't some kind of spiritual road service designed to get us back on the highway. Far from it. With the rosary, Our Lady shows us that, in fact, it is all right to abandon our cars altogether. Because our final destination—the place of rest and renewal we have been trying to get back to all of our lives but can never quite seem to find when we take our directions from the prevailing culture—is only a few paces . . . only a few beads away.

To walk on the Earth is to embrace the Earth
and draw from it everything you need.
Any human being on the planet today
can take off their shoes and stand in the dirt
and instantly know everything there is to know.

Ashes, Ashes, We All Fall Down

At its most basic the rosary is like a children's toy, its prayers a nursery rhyme. Watch a child delight in playing cat's cradle with a piece of string, humming to herself, and it is easy to see the possibility for absorption, imagination, and joy that Our Lady offers us with her beads. Children delight in doing the same things over and over. There is reassurance in repetition, and wonder in the infinite variations of the familiar. To a child no two autumn leaves are the same.

Nor is there any need for artificial seriousness or enforced silence when children play. In one traditional game each child tries to be as quiet and still as possible . . . but no one ever can, because someone inevitably bursts out laughing at the absurdity of it all. Similarly, when we pray the rosary, there is no need to adopt any particular attitude of composure. We grab hold of our beads and, wherever we are, however we are, we laugh if we need to, cry if we must, stop to answer the doorbell, or simply fall into reverie as our minds relax into our hearts again.

The world is a circle that revolves like a spinning top. The seasons are the same. Everything turns. Watch children holding their arms out wide, going round and round until they grow dizzy and collapse, only to get up and do it all over again. Through such spontaneous, lighthearted play, they explore some of the most mysterious truths about our lives.

In the school yard children link hands and dance together in a circle.

> *Ring-a-round the rosie,*
> *A pocket full of posies,*
> *Ashes! Ashes!*
> *We all fall down!*

In older versions, the third line reads "*Ah-tchoo! Ah-tchoo!*" indicating a sneeze. This detail gave rise to the modern belief that the rhyme originated at the time of the Black Death. But there is no record of that interpretation prior to World War II. Still, there is something ominous in the postwar version of the rhyme—*Ashes! Ashes! We all fall down*. It is easy to understand why grown-ups who had lived through the horrors of the Holocaust and the detonation of the first nuclear bombs might have felt some disquiet on watching their children enact this age-old dance, laughing and rushing pell-mell in a circle, only to fall dead at the end of the game.

Nineteenth-century ethnographers assumed that the rhyme originated from a pagan ritual in which children took turns standing at the center of a circle while the others danced about them. The child at the center was the *rosie*, or rose tree, to whom the children all curtsied at the end of the song. In modern days, unfortunately, no one stands in the center of the circle. It's not that the Lady has vanished from her garden. Rather, we have forgotten the point of the game.

When we pray the rosary, we acknowledge Our Lady's place in the circle of the world again. Round and round we go—holding hands, laughing, curtsying, falling down, only to get back up again and start the game anew. There is no end to the story of a soul, just as there isn't any beginning.

This is a universal curriculum that takes the time it takes.
It is not bounded by one lifetime.
It doesn't stop at death.

Our Only Hope

ANYONE WHO HAS EVER SPENT TIME WITH ANY ADDICT knows how heartbreakingly delusional their hopes can be. They are determined to believe they can get their compulsions under control. They'll cut back and indulge only on the weekends, or only in the evenings, or only after a particularly stressful day at work. Even when everyone else can see clearly that they are destroying their lives, addicts cling to the hope that they won't have to stop.

Our relationship to civilization as modern people is much the same. Those of us who live in developed nations love the ease and comfort of our current way of life, not to mention its seeming safety and security. We love electric lighting, inexpensive clothing, and grocery stores with food from all over the world. We depend on the conveniences of jet travel, cheap gas, and email. We don't just enjoy the comfort of air conditioners and the distractions of television; at this point, we need them. We are quick to extol the value of our many technological innovations—and less comfortable examining what they have cost us. Like the addict, we have arranged our lives in such a way that the truth has a hard time getting through.

We don't want to look too closely at where our food comes from—from the horrors of factory farming to the chemical ravages of industrial agriculture. We choose not to notice the toxic landfills, the mountains blasted apart from mining, or the waterways poisoned by the very medicines we think are healing us. We will recycle meticulously and make sure that our appliances are energy efficient. But don't try to tell us that alternative forms of energy are all, in one way or another, dependent on petroleum products, or that virtually *nobody* on the planet knows what to do with the radioactive waste from nuclear power plants.

Ours is the rising anxiety of a culture hell-bent on ecocide. That is why we need so many different drugs to medicate us and electronic devices to distract us just to make it through an ordinary day. We don't want to stop. Meanwhile we hope that some soon-to-be-discovered technology will miraculously clean up all the many messes we have made. But that is the hope of the addict—that we can go on forever as we have, despite the evidence that it is killing us.

The first great revelation of AA came when its founder, Bill Wilson, admitted that he was powerless over alcohol; there was no way he would ever stop drinking on his own. He came to believe that only a power greater than himself could restore him to sanity, and so he let go of his addiction and took hold of that Higher Power instead. Only then was he finally able to get sober after so many years of destroying his health, his marriage, and his career.

But letting go is only truly possible when there is something else that we can hold on to. That is the power of the rosary. To pray the rosary is to put our faith in the Earth again. To pray the rosary is to trust her, and the plants and animals themselves, to show us, bead by bead, what we need to do to get sober.

Coming to terms with what we have done is not going to be easy. Recovery means acknowledging all the pain that our addiction has caused other beings. That certain heartbreak is what frightens addicts most. How do we make amends? How do we take responsibility for the suffering we have caused? How do we find our way back to the garden of the world?

The good news is that we don't have to do that work alone. If the fundamental state of the addict is isolation from others, what offers lasting healing is being in community again—especially with others who are willing to admit what they have done and who they want to be. The hope of the sober is that healing is possible, and that a new life very different from the one we were committed to before can grow from the ashes of our sorrows.

Don't hold the reins.
Don't hold the steering wheel.
Don't hold the strap.
Don't steer.
Hold Me.

Pray for Us Sinners

People are often rankled by the word *sinners* in the traditional version of the Hail Mary. The word has been misused so often that we are apt to mistrust it. Sometimes it is a weapon, and sometimes it is a way of exonerating us of responsibility and the obligation to make amends. I couldn't help myself. The Devil made me do it.

There are saner ways of coming to terms with the pain we have caused to others and to ourselves. There are reconciliation movements, 12-step groups, mediations, interventions, and therapy. What no religious or spiritual program seems to have considered, however, is our sins against the Earth. Until recently, these have rarely registered on the human moral scale.

Some version of the Golden Rule—"Do unto others as you would have them do unto you"—appears in virtually all of the world's major religions. And yet, it never occurs to us to apply that rule to the planet itself.

But breaking the Green Rule creates the very conditions that lead us to break the Golden Rule in the end. Ecological devastation is usually the precursor of violence against one another. Our sins against the Earth have a way of coming home to roost. Carbon gases lead to climate change . . . which leads to drought . . . which leads to hunger . . . which leads to civil unrest and often civil war. Sadly, even our best efforts to love others of our kind are doomed to failure when we fail to love the planet. Which makes honoring our relationship with the Earth the only true antidote to sin.

In the end, it all comes down to our Mother and the violence we commit against her. Our planet provides the air we breathe, the food and water we consume, and virtually everything else we need for life. But for millennia now, we have lived in our heads as a species, convinced that nature would give way indefinitely before the advancement of human ambition. Our bodies tell another story. We are completely dependent on the Earth's bounty for our existence.

Eliminate one half of that bounty, and pretty soon the Golden Rule, for all the beauty and nobility of its conception, won't be able to save us from our "sins." Current projections indicate that, as a direct result of climate change and other anthropogenic factors, up to 50 percent of all plant and animal species on Earth will likely become extinct by century's end—an eventuality that led Stephen Meyer to ask in the closing chapter of his 2006 book, *The End of the Wild*: "What is the essence of our own morality if it fails to encompass most of life on Earth?"

That is why the Hail Mary reads the way it does, "Pray for us sinners." Not me. Not you. *Us*.

The word *sinner* has long been a way of dividing people from one another, and hiding our separation from Nature. The remedy is to accept our collective responsibility for the mistakes of our species against the Earth. It is only when we have truly admitted the harm we have caused to the world around us that we can find a lasting peace among ourselves and recover the joy we have lost.

There is one delusion at the bottom
of human experience today:
the belief that you live in a Motherless,
comfortless world.
This is the source of all other delusions,
and the cause of all unhappiness.

Back to the Forest

THE OLDEST WRITTEN STORY IN THE WORLD DESCRIBES the destruction of a cedar grove sacred to the goddess Ishtar at the hands of a conquering hero. Gilgamesh, the King of Ur, uses the great trunks of that leveled forest to build a temple to his god, thereby gaining everlasting fame. When Ishtar hears of this desecration, she sends the Bull of Heaven to destroy Ur. But Gilgamesh slays the beast, further consolidating his power over the world's first great city-state.

Memorable as it may be as a story of heroism, the real message of the *Epic of Gilgamesh* is that civilization can arise only when the forest has been vanquished. The groves of Asherah would be obliterated by Yahweh in the Bible. The mighty oaks of the Druids would be leveled by the Romans. Colonialism would greatly extend the range of the destruction until, finally, capitalism would ensure the death of most of the great woodlands of the world. Lost were not just the trees but completely different ways of being with the Earth. From empire to empire, continent to continent, the sacred groves of the Lady were obliterated and the Divine Feminine suppressed.

What we have done to the Earth, we have done to women as well. Just as the wild places were plundered, cultivated, and burned, the wild women were veiled, stoned, and tied to the stake as witches. If land could become property and forced into fertility, so could women be exchanged as commodities, their bodies and their children owned by their husbands. The impulse to control and regulate women's sexuality is as old as civilization.

The earliest farmers probably weren't aware of that impulse arising within them as they cultivated the land. They only knew that farming left them more numerous, more powerful, and (seemingly, at least) more secure. But it was impossible to coerce the land into a state of monotony and perpetual productivity without eroding their respect for the sacred feminine, and that soul erosion eventually led them to suppress the Earth and women both.

Of all issues related to ecological collapse, overpopulation is the most controversial. Even some of the most sincere religious defenders of the Earth are reluctant to discuss a woman's right to sex education and birth control, much less her right to sexual pleasure. Yet study after study suggests that when women are given the opportunity to manage the fertility of their own bodies, they do so in ways that benefit not only their own lives but the lives of the plants and animals in their ecosystems. The rights of women and the rights of the Earth are one.

Even more radical is the notion that Our Lady knows what is best for her own body—that the soil knows which weeds will restore its vitality, that the trees have a better idea than human beings what it would take for the forests to return. In 2003, what was then the largest blackout in U.S. history was caused by "unpruned foliage." Overgrown branches brushed against a main power line in Ohio and brought down the grid across the Midwest, the Northeast, and parts of Canada. To us that seemed like a problem; to the trees it was the solution.

Can we tolerate the disruptions to our modern way of life that are inevitably required if the Earth is to heal herself? Can we let the forests reclaim our parking lots and expressways? Can we allow the rivers to find their own way? Can we accept that there may need to be fewer of us, many fewer, if we are to continue as a species? When we pray the rosary, we learn to place our trust in Our Lady—and ultimately to trust her with herself.

Having more trees is more important
than having more people.
Trees can live without people,
but people cannot live without trees.

Mother-Nature

MOST OF US CRAVE MOTHERING—THE SHOULDER TO CRY on, the soup when we're sick, the shared laughter, that little bit of juicy gossip and, from time to time, the good kick in the behind. Mothers grow things and cook things. They birth babies and close the eyes of the dead. Mothers are the ones who show up with casseroles when there is a calamity. And not just mothers, but grandmothers, too. They are the keepers of the old stories and the lost lore.

Yet few people, even parents, aspire to be motherly anymore—much less *grand*motherly. *Motherly* means dowdy, fussy, nosy, and probably a bit old-fashioned. It's become a derogatory term that says more about the ways that women, and women's ways of being, are devalued in our culture. Still, in most institutions, religious or otherwise, there is usually someone, slightly removed from the chain of authority, who hangs out in the kitchen and offers a friendly ear and a little something sweet when we really need it. You can mock that person, or ignore her, but you can't do without her.

The rosary is the story of a woman's journey through the joys and sorrows of motherhood, but it is also an invitation, for both men and women, to get to know the Mother directly by entering into her experience and seeing the world from her point of view. Gradually, as we do that, we begin to trust her with our most intractable problems and dilemmas, along with our barely acknowledged desires. We bring to Our Lady everything that is in our hearts, and we trust that she will take care of us in ways that we could not have imagined.

We begin, too, to recognize those people in our lives who manifest her generosity and her wisdom. It's the gutsy, outspoken woman without any kids of her own who fights tooth and nail for the drug treatment program in her town. It's the man who organizes a string of protests against a lumber company and somehow manages to save a stand of old-growth trees. It's the friend who always intuits when we're in trouble and instinctively knows when to call. The more we begin to trust the rhythms of the beads, the easier it is to let ourselves, man or woman, become the mothers the world needs us to be.

And who is to say that Our Lady, in the midst of caring for the world and everything in it, does not need us as well to be mothers? Perhaps that is why she often appears in the guise of a young girl—to awaken in our hearts the power of our own motherliness . . . for ourselves, for one another, and for the Earth.

It seems like there are mothers
and children in the world—
but there are only Mothers.
The truth is, there are only Mothers.

Rosary Wisdom

ROSARY WISDOM TENDS TO GROW SLOWLY, BUILDING GRADually over the course of a lifetime. The rosary isn't a degree program. There are no classes or courses. There's no diploma at the end. There isn't any end. We never stop accumulating the wisdom of the rosary. The beads turn, the seasons pass. The experiences of a lifetime settle within us like fallen leaves and flowers, becoming the topsoil that nourishes and informs our lives.

Eventually we know instinctively that this is so. We learn to trust that simple knowledge, and after that we always know what to do. But not because we are shrewd or clever. Or because we have become subtle or nuanced in our thinking. We "know things" because we are connected to our Mother. We know things because of the cumulative wisdom of countless mothers in the soil beneath our feet. For with its mix of root and rhizome, dirt and dormant seed, that soil is a form of wisdom all its own. Matter is *Mater*—and that Mater is durable, perennial, and very, very wise. Praying the rosary becomes a way of learning to go barefoot in our souls.

Wisdom comes to us naturally as we pray—for our daily needs, for protection, for right livelihood, for health and happiness, for the healing of friends and family members who suffer from sadness, sickness, or loss.

If we pray the rosary each morning or evening, and gather regularly to pray it with others, we don't have to seek out a spiritual master to find wisdom. We don't have to enroll in a seminary or join a monastery. We pray our maters and paters and follow the circle of the seasons, and wisdom comes to us. Eventually, provided we remain connected to the inevitable cycles of beginnings and endings that are the raw stuff of life, the wisdom of those "circles" takes up residence within us the way that a tree accumulates rings beneath its bark, one for every year.

There is no way to force wisdom, just as there is no way to force the seasons. There is no way to compel our Mother to make us wise faster than our years. The rosary makes us wise because the rosary makes us patient. The seed of wisdom is sown within us from the first moment we take up the beads. It may take a while before we can feel it stirring. In the meantime, we learn to trust that it is so.

Deep in the memories of each of My children
I have hidden all that they need to know.
You need never worry that you will not
know what to do.
My hand is there in the dark
for you to take it.
My presence and My comfort
have been with you from the moment
you first drew breath.

There are many things to learn in life
but only one thing to remember:
I stand waiting in your hearts,
and I will speak if you will listen
and tell you all that you need to know.

The Eternal Return

A SINGLE MOLECULE OF WATER CAN TRAVEL FROM THE depths of the ocean to the heights of the atmosphere. It can become vapor in a cloud, crystallize into a snowflake, or fall to Earth as rain. It can freeze, thaw, pool, and penetrate the Earth as moisture, renewing the life of a forest in the spring. And yet, throughout all of these transformations, it never stops being what it is.

Water is life, they say—which means that water is necessary for life. But if the bodies of living beings are mostly water, isn't the water itself alive? Our bodies don't have water in them the way a vase does. Empty the water from a vase and it is still a vase. Empty the water from a living body and it is no longer alive. Water is the soul of a living planet. When astronomers look for life on other planets, it's water they look for first.

It would take an infinite life span to observe the path of a water molecule as it passed through all of its incarnations. Even then, how would you know where to start? Who can say where a water molecule begins or ends? It moves in cycles too large for the eye to take in. Its age cannot be known.

Our souls, too, journey through vast cycles, like water moving from one body to the next. They don't come and go any more than the water does. Nor can a body possibly contain a soul for long. The body runs out eventually. It ages, falls prey to accident or disease, and finally returns to its Mother. But the soul? Like water, the soul does not die. And like water, it won't stay put. Its nature is to journey, to be always on pilgrimage. It is always seeking and finding its way.

A river requires no belief. Water is its own testimony. It falls and rises, departs and returns, and somehow it is always there—above us, below us, around us, within us. Forever is bigger than one body. The soul has no beginning, no middle, and no end.

The first roads were not roads but rivers.
A road goes where you make it go,
a river goes where it wants to
and teaches you where to go.
When a river goes over a cliff,
it's only a waterfall,
and then the river flows on again.

Don't Fall! *Leap!*

WHAT DO WE DO WHEN WE COME TO THE END OF THE road and there *isn't* any more road? What happens when the farmlands turn to dust, our aquifers run dry, and the wildfires can't be contained? There are those who prefer not to ask such questions, including many of our leaders. But even those who are willing to ask them don't have answers—or, if they do, the answers require changes to our way of life that aren't likely to be implemented anytime soon.

The Miracles of Our Lady of Rocamadour tells the story of a knight who has been captured and placed in a dungeon. Bound in manacles, his predicament is dire. Then he remembers the Lady who grants clemency to the despised, the despairing, and the destitute and utters an ardent, heartfelt prayer to the Virgin.

Filled with faith in her miraculous powers, the knight mounts a daring escape from the dungeon and finds his way to the top of the castle tower, where he jumps from a window and lands, unhurt, on the ground. Now his escape has been noticed, however, and he must quickly flee for his life. Ducking through the door of a church just ahead of his pursuers, he climbs into the rafters and there finds an iron implement with which to break himself free of his chains—but, alas, the guards are now gathered in great numbers below him.

"Then the good knight poured his heart out in prayer once more," says the story, "and cast himself suddenly into the midst of his enemies from above. And what did the Mistress of Mercy do? What help did she provide to her knight, who trusted in her rather than presuming that his own strength would be enough to subdue his enemy? Did she not hold back the knight's assailants? Indeed, she made their legs sluggish and their grasp weak. Thus, he was able to escape from his foes."

The knight's tale is not unusual as far as medieval miracle stories go. Such stories often record astonishing eleventh-hour deliverances. And yet, with its towers and churches (institutional structures that hold no safety and offer no solutions), there is something in this one that makes it almost a parable for the modern age.

Faced with a problem with no discernible solution, the knight prays to Our Lady and, through faith, is given the courage to attempt the impossible. But no sooner has he accomplished one impossible feat than he is faced with the need for another. Twice he attempts a vertical escape from his predicament, and twice he discovers the flaw in his strategy: The way out is not up, but *down*.

Finally, on the second try, the knight prays again as he did at the beginning of his adventure and discovers a trust far more radical than he had before. If his jump from the tower was a calculated risk undertaken because he had no other option, his jump from the rafters is a deliberate choice: a faith-filled leap into the void.

The knight doesn't know how he will be delivered from his captors any more than we know how to make it through climate change. But there is a crucial difference between him and us. He fully acknowledges the impossibility of his situation. There comes a moment when he says, "I'm not going to figure this out. There's no way I can make it out alive on my own."

That, really, is the moment of truth—when the knight acknowledges to himself that it is better to leap than to fall. But that is a hard lesson, and one that comes only at the very end. The rosary prepares us to receive that lesson, but we must be holding it in our hand when that moment inevitably arrives.

And so I answer the question
that each of you is already asking
in the depths of your heart:
"How is this to go on?"
The answer is, it cannot.
Your way has come to an end.
But Mine has just begun.

Expect a Miracle

Around the world today millions of people still wear a small devotional pendant known as the Miraculous Medal, so called because many miracles have been attributed to it. On the front of the medal is Mary standing on a globe with a serpent under her foot. On the back is a curious monogram with two hearts beneath it, one for Jesus and one for Mary, surrounded by a circle of twelve stars. But few who wear the Miraculous Medal know the full story of its origin, or the secret of its power.

In the spring of 1830, a semiliterate nun of twenty-four entered the Convent of Rue du Bac in Paris. From the beginning, Catherine Labouré was considered utterly unremarkable by her peers. And yet, not three months into her novitiate, she witnessed an apparition that changed how people saw the Virgin and conceived of her role in the world.

What few people know today, however, because it is suppressed in nearly all modern accounts of the apparitions, is that in the beginning Catherine did not believe that the figure she had seen was, in fact, the Virgin Mary. "I am not able to say why," Catherine later told her confessor, "but it still seemed to me that it was not she whom I saw." The apparition so defied the young nun's pious expectations of who Mary was, or ought to be, that she had to be told three times by the angelic figure who accompanied the apparition that this, indeed, was what the Virgin really looked like.

One night a few months later, as Catherine was praying in the chapel, the Virgin appeared again. This time she stood above the altar inside of an oval frame that rotated, showing first one side and then the other. On the front Mary stood with her arms outstretched and her hands open. On her fingers were jeweled rings of various colors emitting rays of light that shone down upon the world. These, Mary explained, were the graces she granted in answer to people's prayers. When Catherine asked why some of the rings did not emit light, the apparition answered: "Those are the graces for which people forget to pray."

Whatever reservations Catherine may have had about the woman she encountered in the initial apparition, they had disappeared by then. The figure on the Miraculous Medal is the Virgin Mary that any good Christian would recognize. And yet, embedded in the medal's design (not too subtly, it turns out) are clear signs that this Virgin was far older and more powerful than it would seem.

The most obvious sign is the shape of her body. On the original medal approved by Catherine, the Virgin stands with her arms open, holding wide the rich interior of her robe. That robe forms what are unmistakably the folds of a labia, making the Virgin's whole body a great vulva, the opening to the cosmic womb. Is that image "hidden" in the Miraculous Medal? If so, it is hidden in plain sight. That may be why, in recent years, images of this Virgin have been adapted by feminist artists as a way of reclaiming their own sexual power and independence.

And then, of course, there is the serpent. According to the Bible, Mary ought to be crushing its head as a symbol of "her victory over evil." But on the medal her bare foot rests lightly on its back, not on its head. It could easily turn to bite her if it wanted to, but rather, the snake seems relaxed—as if it has resumed its rightful place as the Goddess's ancient ally.

But it is the back of the medal that holds the biggest surprise. The central image is a monogram: the letter *M* with a crossbar through the middle supporting an upright cross (†M). Bizarrely, and completely unremarked upon by modern scholars, the lower half of that symbol turns out to be the cuneiform word for Inanna (𒈹), the Sumerian "Queen of Heaven." The first cuneiform tablets were not translated until much later in the nineteenth century, and so there was no way that Catherine, even if she had been educated, which she most definitely was not, could have understood what she had seen.

Our Lady is nothing if not wily and more than a little bit subversive. One moment she's Inanna, the next she's Mary. How she must have smiled as she revealed herself to this modest, unassuming nun, knowing that the Church elders would mint her image, little realizing what it was.

Would Church authorities have withdrawn the medal from circulation had they discovered it? Possibly. But the Miraculous Medal proved so "miraculous" that this would quickly have become impossible. People began reporting unexpected cures, overturned convictions, reunions, and last-minute rescues—all of which they attributed to the medal. The Queen of Heaven was generous with her favors. And for reasons everyone could sense, but no one could quite articulate, people loved wearing her image around their necks.

But what are the graces that we forget to pray for? Is there anything that we think is beyond Our Lady's power? Miracles are miracles because they lie outside of what we believe is possible. The Miraculous Medal tells those who wear it that the only limit on what they can pray for is their own imagination.

Mary herself imposes no limits on the graces she is ready to bestow upon us. She is the wild card of karma, the loophole in the cosmic law. The rays of light falling from her fingers; the frank, open stance; the serpent resting beneath her foot—everything about the medal proclaims that power. It says to the faithful: I am your Mother, so be brave and confident. Expect a miracle. Any miracle. Push the limit, and test the power of prayer.

I am speaking to you from an older place.
The reason I have chosen to appear here,
at this time and in this way,
is not to speak from outside of the Catholic Church.
I need to speak from before it.

PART V

QUEEN OF HEAVEN AND EARTH

The Long Story

THE MORE CLARK AND I LEARNED ABOUT THE ROSARY, the more we longed to go to France—not only to visit the statues of the various Black Madonnas and the apparition sites we'd read about, but to see where some of the oldest goddess figurines in the world had been found. We both had the feeling that there was some obscure, long-forgotten pilgrimage we needed to make.

So when the book I'd written with the psychic was unexpectedly optioned in Hollywood, we knew exactly what we were going to do with the money. As if to confirm our intuitions, my film agent celebrated the deal by taking me to Venice Beach . . . to the Rose Café, which turned out to be on Rose Avenue. We arrived to find a giant outdoor mural of a *hamsa* surrounded by angels with eyes all over their wings. Not only that, but both kids were settled in college and Sophie's health was briefly stable. "After twenty-three years of marriage, we are finally going to get a honeymoon!" I texted Clark.

That's how we found ourselves in the Dordogne, a fairy-tale realm in southwestern France full of pretty villages, winding rivers, medieval castles, and limestone caves where evidence has been found of hominids from well over three hundred thousand years ago.

That first morning we drove our rental car along a road that followed a twisting river past vineyards and walnut orchards. Cliffs with deeply worn outcrops that marked the higher water levels of an infinitely remote aeon rose above us on either side. Eventually we reached the edge of a cow pasture where we had arranged to meet our guide.

Christine Desdemaines-Hugon was a former painter turned archaeologist. A beautiful, vibrant woman in her early sixties, she combined the scientist's factual rigor with an artist's intuitive perceptions. She got into our car with a plastic bucket filled with flashlights, a coil of heavy rope, and a Neanderthal hand ax from seventy thousand years ago, which she'd found in her garden, and which she let us hold.

Christine explained to us that the first archaeologists to visit these painted caves, more common than country churches along the Dordogne and Vézère Rivers, had initially assumed that the multitude of animal scenes they discovered were all about the hunt. In fact, there is little evidence that this is so. The artists, who are as likely to have been women as men, depicted the creatures of their world with lifelike precision in all kinds of attitudes and situations, few of them about killing or being killed. In one cave a family of mammoths gathers protectively around a small calf, the hints of smiles on their upturned mouths. In another, a red deer gently licks the bowed forehead of his mate. One remarkable carved tableau depicts bison, lions, and horses—all gathered around a pregnant mare.

Christine suggested that the images may have had a symbolic as well as a representational meaning. Was the baby mammoth like the lamb in a Christian painting? Was the pregnant mare a mother goddess about to give birth? That might explain the almost mythic repetition of certain images, but at this point, tens of thousands of years later, it is impossible to know for sure.

At a number of the state-owned caves, a cheerful, very round French girl was responsible for leading us through the passageways into the inner chambers. We were surprised and delighted when she kept reappearing, hurrying up the path to be ready to greet us and take our tickets at the next stop. She was no paleontologist, but she'd been born in the region and, for years, had spent every day in the company of these images. "What can you tell us about the people who once lived here?" I asked her in my halting French. "Based on these paintings, what do you think they were like?"

I was expecting a textbook answer—that they were human beings just like us, with the same level of intelligence, the same basic skills and interests. So I was surprised when tears welled up in her eyes and she had to brush them away.

"*Joie!*" she said at last. "They knew what joy was," she continued in English. "A joy we do not know anymore, a joy that we have lost."

For these people, that joy was centered within the Earth. They weren't building towers to the heavens as symbols of human ambition. They sought out the natural wombs within the land itself, sometimes crawling for hundreds of yards before reaching an inner chamber. There, by lamplight, they found the flickering shapes of animals already inhabiting the natural contours of the rock. Using charcoal and ocher—sometimes only a fingertip if the limestone was wet and soft—they joined their Mother in the work of creation, coaxing her animals to life. These were a people who still knew where they came from. A people who still knew where they belonged. No wonder they felt so much joy.

Christine pointed out how little the style, location, and subject matter of the art had changed over vast expanses of time. Tens of thousands of years might pass and still these people, the first *Homo sapiens* in central Europe, would be painting mammoths and lions in the exact same way, in the exact same places under the Earth. To modern people obsessed with novelty and innovation, it can be easy to see their culture as impossibly stagnant. It is more difficult to acknowledge its radical sustainability.

For our final cave, Christine directed us back to the parking area where we'd originally met her. We had come full circle. The cows had broken out of their enclosure now and were standing next to her car. A small old man, a local farmer wearing a beret and chewing on the filter of his cigarette, ambled over to us. He handed a set of keys to Christine so that we could visit Bernifal, a cave located on his land and privately owned by his family.

Together we walked up a dirt path through a forest of hornbeams and chestnut trees, shuffling through fallen yellow leaves. It was late in the day and the light was golden and heavy. Christine unlocked a green metal door built right into the ground, and we stepped into the darkness. Because this was not a state-sponsored site, there was no artificial lighting for safety purposes. Christine knew that Clark had written a book about the lost experience of darkness and was happy to let us wait in silence, feeling the blackness envelop us.

After a minute or so, she flicked on her flashlight, wiggling her fingers over the lens to give it the quality of a flickering flame. Not only did the original artists use the natural rock formations to give a sculptural quality to their work, when these rock animals were illuminated by lamplight, they often seemed to move. But all that we had seen up until now left us completely unprepared for what we witnessed when Christine removed her fingers from her flashlight and brought the beam to rest on a spot of cave wall a foot or two above our heads.

Apart from handprints, there is little human presence in any of the caves. Those images of *Homo sapiens* that exist are mostly stick figures drawn without any of the anatomical precision or artistic sophistication that characterize the portraits of animals. But here, at Bernifal, a face gazed back at us through the darkness of time that was so realistic, and so clearly a portrait of a specific individual, it took our breath away.

"She's from the Magdalenian era, during the last Ice Age, roughly fifteen thousand years ago, the time of the great reindeer hunters and an explosion of art," explained Christine. "If it *is* a she, that is. Sometimes I think it's a woman and sometimes a man. I don't know. You can see the topknot of her hair."

When we'd begun studying prehistory, Clark and I had both experienced the same confusion about the "Magdalenian era" that we'd never resolved.

"What does that period have to do with Mary Magdalene?" I asked Christine.

"Nothing at all," she answered. "The Magdalenian era is named for the Site Madeleine, a rock shelter where the first artifacts of the period were unearthed."

"Ah!" said Clark and I together. "That explains it." Only it didn't. Madeleine was French for Magdalene. But where had the rock shelter gotten its name from?

Christine moved her flashlight away from the face to show us how a stalagmite, when lit from behind, cast a penetrating shadow into a large cleft in the rock. Pouring out of that womblike shape was a profusion of woolly mammoths. "Doesn't leave much to the imagination!" she said, laughing.

There were other things to see in the cave—ocher handprints, mysterious dot markings called "tectiforms," and another pregnant mare. But both of us wanted to gaze at the face again. For a long time we stared at her, feeling her look back at us. Until finally, it was time to leave the cave.

We were quiet on our way back through the forest to the car. Of the many sacred places we had visited in our lives, this surely was the holiest. I believe these people almost certainly wanted us to find their pictures. Here is joy, they were saying, here in the darkness, in the Earth. If one day you ever forget that, we will have left a reminder for you, a way back to the world that you have lost.

As we said goodbye, we told Christine that we were headed the next day to the shrine of Our Lady of Rocamadour. She was appalled. She couldn't believe we were going to waste our time in France on such a worthless site. "It's architecturally so uninteresting. Besides, it's a tourist trap," she told us. "There'll be buses everywhere. Little shops selling plastic souvenirs. You two are going to hate it." She tried to convince us to spend time visiting some other caves.

We were reluctant to explain our devotion to Our Lady. We certainly didn't mention that Clark was in the habit of speaking with her. We've often wished we had an easy way to say, "No, we're not Catholic, we're not even religious, but we do recognize Our Lady as real—as real as the Earth, and as real as our mothers . . . only in an ecofeminist kind of way." We just said that we liked visiting Black Madonnas.

"She's not as old as they say she is, you know," scoffed Christine.

A thick fog shrouded the valley the following morning. On our way to Rocamadour we passed through towns so small that the signs saying we were entering and leaving them were scarcely a hundred meters apart. The climb was gradual until near the end when, after a series of turns that left us feeling like we'd been blindfolded and spun around, we came out atop a long ridge that gave way eventually onto a narrow plateau. Just when we thought we must be lost, we found ourselves in Rocamadour.

Apart from a small church, a château, and a somewhat less-than-ancient-looking graveyard, there wasn't much to distinguish it. A tourist center. Souvenir shops. A few restaurants. The streets were practically empty. It had begun to drizzle.

We parked the car. In truth, we were disappointed. Christine had been right. Wondering where we'd find the chapel of the Black Madonna, we stopped a middle-aged woman carrying groceries, who pointed us down a cobblestone street so narrow it was almost an alleyway.

We had just emerged from between a series of low buildings when the fog suddenly lifted and we discovered that the road we'd been walking on, which was beginning a steep descent, skirted the edge of a precipice. I reached out instinctively to clutch Clark's hand. The height was dizzying. A falcon circled in the air above us. The river, a tributary of the Dordogne, wound through the valley far below. And there, nestled on a cliff between the water and the sky, was the medieval village where the chapel was.

Clark and I have often joked that the Glorious Mysteries of the rosary are a bit of a roller-coaster ride. Jesus ascends, the Holy Spirit descends, Mary is made Queen of Heaven and, at last, Queen of the Earth. Up and down, up and down. Our pilgrimage to Rocamadour mirrored these rhythms. We'd driven up and up to the plateau, then walked down and down to the village. Now we had to climb 216 steps, worn by the feet of centuries of pilgrims, to get to the chapel itself, which seemed almost to hang in midair.

I kept my eyes focused on my feet while Clark reported on the extraordinary views. I only looked up once we'd reached the small square in front of the chapel. No one else was there. Maybe it was the rain earlier that day, or perhaps it was some arrangement of Our Lady's, but we had the Chapelle Miraculeuse to ourselves. Votive candles filled the tiny, dim sanctuary. Whoever had lit them had come and gone. The walls were covered in small plaques thanking the Lady for her miracles. POUR LES ENFANTS. MERCI MARIE, 1855. The strangest discovery of all was that this very date had once been the feast day of Our Lady of Rocamadour.

As often happened while we were in France, we had the sense of following an older map, as if our feet were remembering things our heads had forgotten. One moment we were tourists fumbling with a guidebook. The next we were pilgrims putting one foot in front on the other, trusting Our Lady to guide the way.

The Black Virgin of Rocamadour herself, perched high above the altar against a background of red velvet, was surprisingly small. Made from the dark walnut wood that is everywhere in that region of the world, she has a thin body with long arms and hands, and a wise and homely face. Like Isis, she holds her child facing outward in her lap.

That day she was dressed in a shiny white satin frock especially made for her. Unlike many of France's Black Madonnas, she'd survived the Reformation, the French Revolution, and the march of the Enlightenment, eras in which countless statues of the Virgin were burned and sometimes even beheaded. Perhaps it was because she was so difficult to get to that she had endured through these endless wars of belief. Whatever the explanation, she was a survivor. And, whatever Christine said to the contrary, she was clearly very old.

Though the statue may only date from A.D. 800, even the pious guidebook, created with the cooperation of the local bishop, explains that devotion to Our Lady in this valley goes far back into the distant past. Within walking distance from the chapel is another grotto with paintings of horses, deer, and other animals from more than twenty thousand years ago.

Clark and I lit a candle and sat down in the first row of chairs before the altar. We had brought with us dozens of petitions from our rosary friends back home to read aloud. Clark would read one and we would say a Hail Mary, and then I would read another and we would do the same. People wanted healing, meaningful work, companionship, love. A woman who had lost her four-year-old daughter to a sudden inexplicable illness prayed that Our Lady would send some sign from her child. Another had suffered under the burden of homelessness for the past few years and longed for a place to call her own. Both prayers would be answered.

Clark and I prayed for our daughter, Sophie. We wanted to find a doctor who could tell us once and for all what was the matter with her and what could be done to make her feel better. We wanted her to be healed.

When we finally did meet a doctor who definitively diagnosed Sophie two months later, we knew it was Our Lady's doing. We had been to so many specialists over the years. But the news this woman gave us would turn out to be as much a verdict as a relief. What was making Sophie so sick was an extremely rare connective tissue disorder for which there was no treatment and no cure.

"You're a much older model of human," the doctor explained to Sophie in her office overlooking the Hudson River. "That's the real problem. Your collagen issues make you not only hypermobile, but hypersensitive as well—particularly to the toxins in our environment." It was probably the glut of artificially created products—the plastics, the paints, the pesticides—that had triggered all of her problems. "In a different world, an older world," she told Sophie, "you might have managed just fine."

The answer to one prayer is sometimes the opportunity for another. Life is a pilgrimage, healing is a journey. Now Sophie would need a miracle.

I looked up at Our Lady's rough-hewn face in the chapel that day and I felt that she was gazing directly at me. There was a hint of a smile on her lips, as if she recognized how ridiculous the outfit was that the church had dressed her up in. She was no remarkable work of art crafted by a sculptor of limitless skill. But she was completely alive there in that chapel. No wonder she drew people from all over the world to her like a magnet. Already I knew that wherever I would be in the future, I could turn to the east and feel her kind and loving face gazing back at me.

Clark and I finished praying the rosary and, just as we uttered the last words of the Hail Holy Queen, we looked up to find there were others sitting behind us, their hands clasped in prayer. People were beginning to trickle into the chapel now, but these didn't feel like tourists. I'd read that pilgrims traditionally made two trips to Rocamadour—the first in petition, the second in gratitude. I prayed that one day Clark and I would have reason to return.

After lunch we headed back to our inn along another road, which took us down the front of the cliff. It was no steeper than any mountain road in the Catskills, but I found myself paralyzed with terror. The valley below felt infinitely far away, and I was certain we were going to careen over the edge as we took each hairpin turn. I couldn't believe I was in the grips of my old fears again after all of these years of praying the rosary. I was trembling and could barely breathe. I shut my eyes tight and clutched my rosary beads.

At last we came to a mostly flat area and Clark told me that I could open my eyes. Sheep were grazing in the fields on the edge of a tiny village with a little church dedicated to Our Lady of the Snows. We drove over to the church and parked. Still shaking, I got out of the car, and Clark followed me.

"You're going to offer thanks for not going over the edge of the cliff and dying in a fiery crash, right?" he joked.

"Yes," I snapped, still too traumatized to be amused.

It was a bare little sanctuary in the middle of nowhere, but within it were the same two statues we'd come to expect from every church we entered in France. On one side was St. Anthony tenderly holding the baby Jesus. On the other, Joan of Arc wielded her sword. It seemed to be another one of those sly reminders from Our Lady that men could be motherly and women could be fierce. I lit a candle in front of the statue of the Virgin near the front and sat down in a well-worn wooden pew. I still felt like I was descending the mountain, like I couldn't get out of the car.

"What's the matter with me?" I said out loud.

Clark settled into the pew beside me. He shut his eyes and began to pray the rosary. After a moment, he sighed and shivered the way he does when Our Lady appears to him. For a long time he was quiet, listening. I felt my own nerves begin to calm as a soothing warmth spread through my body.

"Our Lady says," began Clark haltingly, "that . . . that . . ."

"You have just come down from the highest spot on Earth. But the height you have descended from cannot be measured in the or-

dinary way. The height of My chapel at Rocamadour cannot be measured in vertical feet. Its height is the measure of the time that stands below it, time that is millions of years deep.

"Measured in this way, Everest is a foothill in comparison with Rocamadour. You were frightened because I allowed you to experience the depth of your descent. Because I allowed you to witness the true height of time. But there is no reason for distress. Does not that time, deep as it is, support you even now? Is there any cause for you to fear? The whole Earth is a column that supports you—from within as well as from without."

Over the past few years, I had taken to carrying a notebook with me in order to write down the things Our Lady said. In the beginning, her utterances had been brief enough for Clark to remember and record in his pocket notebooks. These days she had extensive guidance to offer, and there was no way he could write it all down.

Sometimes as I wrote I had the sense of my mind being reconfigured to accommodate some new way of thinking—or maybe an old way, long forgotten by our species, that Our Lady was teaching us again. I had that feeling now. Height was a measure not of the space above the ground, but of the depth of time *below* it. It would take lifetimes to understand that. Or it would take an act of surrender. Maybe it was as simple as learning to trust that she was always there—all the way from the aerie at Rocamadour to the grotto of Bernifal.

She had guided the footsteps of those early hominids who left Africa again and again on long-forgotten pilgrimages of their own. She had accompanied us through asteroid impacts, volcanic supereruptions, and more ice ages than we could count. *"You trusted Me then,"* she'd said once, after walking us through a breathtaking series of past apocalypses. "*Will you not also trust Me now?*"

That afternoon, driving back after our stop at the church, Clark and I got turned around and lost. Not that we were particularly worried. There was nowhere else we were supposed to be and each new vista was more beautiful than the last. Every now and then we'd catch glimpses of the river through the trees and, as long as we followed it, we figured we couldn't go very wrong. An enormous flock of chattering geese blocked the road at one point, and we got out to talk with them. That's when Clark saw a sign indicating that "Le Site Madeleine" was only a few kilometers up ahead.

In one of her earliest conversations with us, Our Lady had explained that time and space were more complicated than we understood. She compared them to "paper folds." Space was not flat and time was not linear; rather they were wrapped around each other in a complex origami that was almost impossible to understand but that we have all experienced in one way or another. We get a sense of déjà vu and feel unnerved. We meet a total stranger we're certain we already know. In our dreams a location is both one place and another. We arrive somewhere as if by accident and know it's exactly where we were headed all along.

It was that eerie sense of synchronicity that made us head to the Site Madeleine. We arrived just as it was about to close, but the tired ticket taker assured us we could spend as much time as we wanted in the ancient rock village by the river—although he would be locking the door to the tiny museum in just a few minutes. The other tourists were headed back to their cars as Clark and I quickly studied the exhibits.

We saw a photograph of the famous carving, found in the rock shelter, of a bison stretching his neck back over his shoulder to lick an insect bite on his haunch. We saw all kinds of stone tools and spear points. There was a facsimile on display of the bones of a four-year-old child surrounded by shells in a Paleolithic grave. It turned out that people had lived in the rock shelter beside the river for tens of thousands of years, although it was only in the eighth century that their descendants had carved a "troglodytic village" directly into the limestone above it. But what riveted my attention was a map of the site itself, showing its position on the Vézère River.

The Site Madeleine was located at the end of a circular loop called a "meander." Meanders occur when a river veers away from its original direction, curving round and round until it comes full circle and eventually gets back on course again. If the meander were a rosary, and it looked just like one on the map, the Site Madeleine was located like the last bead, right next to the first.

Weren't the past twelve thousand years of human history a meander? We'd turned off of the long path we'd been on as a species—because of agriculture or the subjugation of women or a myriad of other choices and mistakes. But no matter. Whatever detours we took, we were still part of the river. And the river was always headed to the sea.

At closing time we stepped outside the museum to see the setting sun and the autumn foliage reflected in the water. We walked past a ruined tower at the top of the bluff, all that was left of a former castle, and walked down a short series of steps to find ourselves in a stone village so small it would have fit easily in our backyard. We looked at the empty rooms and were surprised to learn that people had lived here until just over a century ago.

Finally we came to the tiny stone church, a simple room

really, that looked out over the river. We had found the answer to our question about the Magdalenian era. The rock shelter on the river below had been named after the thousand-year-old chapel that stood directly above it: the Church of the Madeleine. Nothing was in it—except for a single statue.

We both recognized her immediately.

She was the exact same size as the small statue of Our Lady that Clark had bought so long ago. She was wearing the exact same headdress, the exact same robes, holding her skirt with one hand in the exact same manner. We'd looked at hundreds of Madonnas over the years and had never seen one that looked anything like her until this moment. The only difference was, instead of holding the world in her other hand, this statue held the alabaster jar of Mary Magdalene. Only it didn't look like a jar, it looked like some kind of tower. Or not a tower exactly, but a column.

One Mary held the world, the other the column of saints.

Hidden in this tiny chapel, abandoned for centuries, was a kind of grail. That this lost Madonna should have also given her name to a lost age, when human beings had the creative joys of culture without the sorrows of civilization, felt strangely appropriate. The ruined castle, the medieval chapel, the stone village, the Paleolithic shelter—all one on top of another at the end of a meander in this valley where human beings had found refuge during another climate catastrophe. None of this felt like a coincidence. It felt like a message.

She was with us, even when we did not know it. Wherever it was that we were going, she was already there.

At the end of the rosary, we crown Our Lady Queen of Heaven and Earth. No longer are these two realms separate. No longer are we banished from Eden. No longer does our story end with hellfire and damnation. The beads slip through our fingers and eventually we arrive at an end that is also a beginning. Life goes on and on.

She will be with us whether we pray the rosary or not. It is important to remember that. Her love comes with no conditions. Not one soul is denied the sanctuary and the sweetness of her embrace. But when we take her hand in ours with the rosary, we acknowledge the eternal pilgrimage of the heart and can experience the comfort and consolation of the long story of our souls.

The Column of Saints

When you hear of a column, normally you think of a structure—something built with tools and made from wood or metal or stone. Its purpose is to elevate, to support a platform or a roof. But the Column of Saints is not that kind of column. It is not something you can build. The Column of Saints builds you. It supports you. It is in your bones, your sinews, and your cells. It is your bones, your sinews, and your cells. And also in the ground beneath your feet.

The Column of Saints is not like a column that supports a church. There is nowhere you can go that you do not stand directly atop it. The whole Earth is a column that supports you—from within as well as from without.

I speak to you with one voice about these matters, but the voices below Me are many. All who have lived, all who are living now, and all who are to come as well—this is the Column of Saints.

This is not an article of religious faith. No one expects you to believe in anything for which you do not feel the power of its presence within you. Your bones support you. You believe in your bones. From your bodies you call forth children, music, art, beauty, good deeds. These emerge from you like flowers. You believe in these things as well.

Step outside and raise your foot. Then bring it down as hard as you can. If your foot goes through the ground as if it were made of air not dirt, then you are free to doubt Me. If not, then do not doubt

Me. I don't monitor your faith. I support you. I am there when you call. So test Me. Pray. Speak to Me about your concerns.

Going forward, I would like you to perform a graft. Whatever your prayer intentions are, whatever your heart's desires, graft them onto the following short prayer. Say to Me, "Lady, are you there? Show me you are there, Mother. Let me feel your presence." Speak to Me as Someone who is present and right beside you.

Sometimes people pray to Me like I'm not there. They speak to Me, but without any real expectation that they will feel My presence in return. That is not the way to pray. Graft your petition onto My actual presence. Know that I am there.

In praying the rosary, you must learn to trust the sun before it rises, and the moon after it sets. There are things you cannot know with your head that you can know with your heart. And there are things your heart cannot know that you can know with your feet. So get grafted. Get grounded.

The Column of Saints stands below you to support you. You will learn everything from the bottom up. Just remember to perform the graft. Talk to Me. I am there.

Giving Birth to Prayer

PEOPLE TODAY BELIEVE THAT PRAYER IS A FORGOTTEN ART, BUT *to believe that is to close your eyes, stop up your ears, and shut the door of your heart against the world. For the Earth and all that is in it—the plants, the animals, the weather, the elements themselves, even those things that you do not think of as possessing life force or volition—all of these without exception are deeply and continuously engaged in prayer.*

Your lungs work, even while you are sleeping. Your heart beats from the moment that you are born. The mists cover the valleys. The rain falls, and the rivers flow. Prayer is the one ceaseless, universal activity. When you take up the beads of the rosary, you are joining with that activity as surely as the sun rises and sets, the moon moves through her phases, and the stars turn in their great wheel around the sky.

You must know that there are no limits on prayer because there was no beginning to prayer. At birth you come in somewhere in the middle of a great story of prayer that, because it forms a circle like the beads of the rosary, is truly without end.

Know that when you pray, your prayers are heard and answered everywhere at once. In truth, prayer doesn't begin anywhere . . . or end anywhere. The prayers you utter flow to you, then through you, then pass beyond you to points elsewhere throughout the world.

You believe that your lives are supported by a monetary economy, but that economy is only an illusion. The world itself is noth-

ing but an economy of prayer. This is what you must learn. This must become your devotion. The world is nothing but prayer.

Prayer makes things happen, but making things happen is not the same as prayer. You have heard people say, "Pray . . . and take action." They never say, "Take action . . . and then pray." You must learn to discern the path ahead through prayer and then follow where prayer leads. How else will you seek your heart's desire? How else will you know that you are free?

There will be times when your actions are limited, when your options are few and your world is narrowed. Even then, to pray first will guide you and show you the possibilities for action that you would otherwise not have imagined. Through prayer you can reunite with the fecundity and creativity of Life itself.

Draw forth from the darkness what is within you so that it may be seen and take on form and color, just as a mother brings forth the child from her womb, and the Earth brings forth flowers. You must give birth to prayer even if you must experience birth pangs, even if it causes you travail. Not to do so is not to carry forth the Life that is within you.

Always know that you were born to bring forth that which is within you into this world, and that work begins, as all things begin, with the Rose.

Footsteps

THERE IS A WISDOM AND AN ORDER IN THE WAY ONE LEAF FALLS *atop another, and together they lie with their backs against the ground, relaxing and easing back into the embrace of the Mother from Whom they came.*

You must always remember that I don't do random, I only do love. When you know this in your heart, you will know that there are no wrong moves so long as you travel on the Path of Faith.

But the Path of Faith is slow and steady—like the trail that is sometimes barely discernible as it passes through a forest or over the grasses of a field. To follow that path requires going at the pace of life and no faster. Most of your problems stem from moving faster than the speed of life. Clouds, mountains, trees, tides, rivers, and streams—all of these without exception move at the pace of life.

The closest you can come as a human to knowing that pace is walking. It was always in walking that you were closest to an understanding of your world. In the past, even your ships were a way of walking, using the power of muscle or wind to cross the waves. But trains, airplanes, and automobiles have no wisdom in them—whatever you might say in their favor. When you were riding on horses or donkeys, oxen or elephants, those animals walked beneath you, so there was still a rhythm to your contact with the Earth. But where is the rhythm of a highway or a rail? Birds have wingbeats, like steps in walking, but aviators and passengers experience nothing of this kind.

If the rhythm of walking guided you then, will it not also guide you now?

I understand that you sometimes don't know what to do in the face of change and uncertainty. But you do know what to do. Everybody does. Just take the next right step. There is deep, old wisdom in this.

Once, walking itself was a conversation with the Earth. There was no difference between living and walking then, no difference between knowing and walking. If you took a wrong step, you could feel it in the soles of your feet.

Know that there is no problem, even now, that cannot be solved by moving at the speed of life—neither faster, nor slower. The rhythm of your footsteps is the heartbeat of the Earth.

The Space Between Stars

In every heart there is a small garden very much like a handful of dirt. Within that dirt is everything needed to grow a miracle. But each heart is distinct; each has its own needs. Some gardens are well tended. Others require weeding. Sometimes there is debris that must be cleared away.

For some hearts, a seed can fall in the soil and instantly take root and pop up. For others, the same seed has to be planted and replanted over a long period of time before it will sprout. You can't always see the seed when it is sprouting and about to send a green shoot up through the soil. So be patient and don't lose hope. Its germination is hidden just under the dirt.

When you say to some people, "Pray for a miracle!" what they hear is "It's never going to happen." Say it to others and they expect to witness something like a fireworks display. Neither is true.

The miraculous and the natural are not at odds with each other. They are one and the same. You must know that when you are praying for a miracle, you are praying for a natural outcome, for the most natural outcome of all. Your understanding of miracles needs to become organic. Then you will understand.

On a night of shooting stars, there is no pattern in the way the meteors flash across the sky. In the same way that you cannot say where or exactly when the next shooting star will appear, you cannot know when or where the miracle will come.

When you dream, you pass into the realm of these shooting

stars. It is likewise when you meditate or pray. Miracles are not performed by daylight. They are not born of the conscious mind. They come from the space between stars—from the dark places you don't think to look. Therefore, they always come as a surprise.

There may be many reasons why one person experiences a miracle right away, while for another the miracle comes only after a great struggle. Both hearts have the dark—or the soil—they need to call forth a miracle. But every heart matures in its own time.

In the meantime, be patient. Pray. Look. Listen. That is all you need to know.

I Will Carry You

FOR A LONG TIME NOW, YOUR ARTISTS AND SCULPTORS HAVE POR-*trayed the protective virtues of My cloak. It is thrown over the shoulders of those in need of shelter. Its warmth comforts those who seek solace. It has been known to conceal those who sought safety from their pursuers or persecutors within its folds. But those paintings and sculptures fail to grasp its true nature.*

If you venture out into the woods at a certain time of year and remain very still, occasionally you will see a mother possum whose babies have grown large enough that they will no longer fit in her pouch and must be placed upon her back as she climbs trees or crosses the stones of a stream. She's a comical sight, with so many small possums all clustered and clinging to her back. They always seem about to fall off. But she never loses them. Between the place where they began and the place where they arrive, her body is their only home.

You have long misunderstood the nature of our relationship. Granted, that misunderstanding served you in certain ways. Seeking My protection under the eaves of churches was your way of staying put. Creating religious institutions in My name allowed you to build towers, build cities, build empires. Going forward, you will not be able to build any of these things. Nor do you have any need of them.

You must understand that you are clothed in My robe by virtue of having a body. Nothing can alter that. Nothing can destroy it.

Nothing can take that away. So you must not seek protection under the eaves of structures and institutions that, even now, are in the process of being destroyed or dismantled.

The robe of My protection is the Earth you stand upon. What your feet touch is none other than the warm body of your Mother. The Earth that rises to meet your footsteps, to support you and carry you forward on your way, is nothing but that mother possum's back.

I will carry you where you must go. There really isn't any other readiness but that. I will take you where you must go.

At birth the umbilical cord is cut and tied off and becomes the navel. But that only happens in your world. I don't experience any such severing. The cord that once connected you to your mother now connects you to the world, which is also your mother. It is as if I have moved you from one hip to the other when you were born—same mother, different hip. I am carrying you just the same.

Dirt to Dirt

PEOPLE SAY THAT THE WORLD IS DYING, BUT I TELL YOU THAT She is pregnant and near to giving birth. So little of what you see and understand about your world is true. You hold the broad outlines of a coming collapse, but you cannot foresee the disappearance of the world that you have made.

Your world is not My world. But My world is yours, and if you will let Me I will lead you there again. All of your fears, all of your worries, all of your anxious preoccupations—these have a single root cause: The world you have made cannot endure, and you cannot foresee the world to come.

If you look only at the distaff, all you see is the unraveling. If you look at the spinner's hands, however, you will see that threads are being made. And if you follow those threads, you will see how they are plaited and woven into cloth. The unraveling will command the attention of those who have no faith. It will become the thing they look at, and for many it will be all that they see.

You must know that nothing is destroyed without something else being created, and you must have faith that this is so. I am taking that which has no value and giving that which is good in return.

Nature does this constantly. What has become spent, what has exhausted its own life force, is taken and used to feed other life. This is like the turning of a spinning wheel. The distaff unravels, but the threads come together. And out of all those threads something new and wonderful is being woven.

When someone dies, at the funeral the priest recites the words "Ashes to ashes, dust to dust . . . For from the dust wast thou taken, and to dust thou shalt return." But ashes do not bring forth bodies, and nothing grows from dust. Already in your ancient scriptures, the soil is dry. The Earth has lost Her vigor.

Think how different it would feel to say, "Dirt to dirt." For dirt is a living thing. You were brought forth from Life, and it is to Life that you return at death. These are the words you should use at the graveside to bury those whom you love.

A Great Wind

THERE'S A STORM OFF IN THE DISTANCE AND THE AIR IS BECOMing charged. *You can feel it. When a great storm is coming, everyone knows it. The animals know it, the plants know it. Even the ground knows it. There is a feeling of expectation, a sense of imminent arrival. But that is only a metaphor. The storm that is coming is bigger than the weather of any particular region. This storm will cover the world.*

The birds know where to go in a storm. The earthworms love a storm. Animals understand the violence of a storm and therefore have no fear of it. But people will rush about.

My advice to you now is to find a place that steadies you—a place that gives you courage, wisdom, and perspective. Each of you knows the place I speak of. Each of you has a place to go that centers you, because that place is your center.

You have been taught to believe that the mind is its own place, and that the world therefore lies within you. In truth, the world lies without. That which you call the "inner world" is fully revealed before you. It is spread out over the whole Earth and you do not see it. There is no difference between yourself and the world.

Once you know this, you will know where your heart is, and you can go to that place to find solace and guidance. Once everyone knew how to find the place of the heart in the world.

Just as water vapor rises from lakes and streams, from the oceans and the land itself, gathering into great clouds in the sky, just so the forces now massing will gather together, coalescing and growing dark until they resolve themselves in a storm.

To wait for that storm to arrive, training your eyes anxiously upon the horizon, is not to understand what a storm is and what it means. A storm is not something that happens to you, but something that happens through you. The wind and your being are one.

That wind is getting underneath everything right now, lifting everything. There is no place it cannot go. No locked door it cannot penetrate. No mind shut so fast that it is proof against the spirit.

No boardrooms are secure. There are no encryptions, no missile silos that can keep it out. There are no treasuries, no seed vaults, no hearts or minds I cannot reach. The doors are about to be opened and the contents of the treasury revealed. I am blowing up the skirts of the world.

A great wind is a great power, and great power is required before you will see My face again. Some things can be seen only when the obstacles to seeing them have been thoroughly removed. That is what great winds are for.

The Shadow of My Protection

AS YOU FACE THE CHALLENGES THAT LIE BEFORE YOU, YOU MUST never ask, "Am I equal to these demands?" Ask rather, "How will I bring forth what I need from the treasury of prayer? How far down into the well of my being must I reach to draw from the reserves of faith and love and wisdom all that I require to successfully complete this journey or this task?"

I set no obstacle before you to defeat you. As a stone in the river raises the level of the water so that it flows over its top, or directs the course of the water toward another path—just so, nothing can withstand the patience and the resourcefulness of prayer. Nothing can defeat the power of prayer.

You will learn this by doing it. Prayer is the only true teacher from one aeon to the next. So have no fear—and never give in or give up. I am praying within you and right beside you, now and forevermore.

There will be times ahead when the path will not be clear and you will not be able to follow it on your own. There will be moments when it seems there is no path to follow at all. In those moments, you must place your hand in Mine and let Me lead you through what you do not understand.

You now walk and act by your own understanding. But there are places where your understanding cannot reach. Some people reach that place and assume that it is the end. But this is not so. The end of your path is the beginning of Mine, but you must walk forward on that new path to claim it and make it your own. To venture forward when you have reached the end of what can be thought, influenced, conquered, or controlled, you must learn to trust Me and let Me lead you by the hand.

Just as you can find shade beneath a great tree, even in the heat of the day, when the sun is at its peak, I can give you peace and solace, rest and renewal, even in the midst of trouble, struggle, and contention. Never concede a fight that you know to be right, and never think in the heat of the moment that you are alone.

I am always with you. You do not exist for yourself alone, nor do you stand alone. Many beings stand with you and beside you. Great forces can be assembled in the moment that you call My name.

The Length of a Soul

THERE ARE NO UNFINISHED LIVES, BECAUSE THERE ARE NO SINgle lives. Life goes on and on. If you knew how many lives there were to work with, you would learn to be patient and know that some things just take time. Lives are being given to you—more lives than you could imagine—over and over again.

Those who learn to manage time gracefully will be happy from one lifetime to the next. Those who are thrown off-balance by time will live with anxiety and confusion. You must know that this is not the only life, and not the only time. You can learn this if you will.

Just as the birds move easily from tree to tree with nothing to block their passage, I can teach you to move freely from one lifetime to the next. With this confidence, much that seems difficult in this lifetime will become possible for you. Healings and reconciliations that seem unlikely can easily be obtained, and the joy that has eluded you can be found close at hand.

You cannot trace the path of your soul from life to life in the same way that you follow your days from week to week, your months from year to year. But know that your lives are longer than you realize, and pray and remain open to the wisdom that is yours. That wisdom is the birthright of having a body.

It is best for this learning, however, not to be anxious or afraid. There is nothing you have now that cannot be given to you again. There is no one you have loved who is forever lost to you. Nor are you condemned to repeat the same mistakes and follies. The long story of your soul is wiser and more generous than you know.

The human concept of the soul is like a shiny coin faceup on the ground. It is flat. The most you can imagine is flipping it over to see what is on the other side. I want to show you the full length and brightness of a soul. I want you to feel its amplitude. It is incalculably long and old. A soul is so much deeper, so much brighter than you imagine. The universe is astounded by every soul. The universe is not big enough to contain a soul.

Know that you can pick up the thread of your own soul in this lifetime the moment you pick up the rosary. So don't lose heart, and never give in to fear. Live with confidence, knowing that there are reasons for all things that happen. You do not live in a random universe because you do not live in a Motherless universe.

You know by now that it was I Who, through your mothers, gave birth to your bodies. Know also that I have given birth to your souls—and a soul may never be destroyed.

An Invitation

Your lives are layered year upon year. The things that you see and do mean one thing when you are young, another in adolescence, young adulthood, and middle age, and yet another when you are old. And yet, in the same way that you accumulate wisdom and understanding over the course of a single lifetime, you accumulate instincts, intuitions, and intimations from one lifetime to the next. Your lives are layered many fathoms deep. It was once the duty of parents and grandparents to initiate you into the long story of your soul.

But the parents and grandparents of the present age instruct you only for the present and the future, having forgotten the vast reservoir of knowledge that lies behind them and below them. They no longer function as parents or grandparents, but rather as brothers and sisters—equally young, naïve, and innocent of time.

You have heard your generals and presidents speak of "surgical strikes." What an odd expression that is, the pairing of surgery with an act of violence, the marriage of medicine and war. What I propose is just the opposite of that: a surgical repair.

The rosary that has come down to you over the centuries is a medical kit to be used on the battlefield that now lies all about you. Make no mistake—this is not the battle between good and evil foretold in your scriptures. The war being fought is between your species and the Earth. That war makes itself felt in every part of My body—from the depths of My womb that you call stone, strata, and sedi-

ment to the fine blue linen of My mantle that you call your atmosphere. This battle is being fought beneath you, above you, and all about you. The deaths are many and the destruction is nearly complete.

When you take up the rosary, you are holding the medicine I gave you long ago, along with the tools for repairing My body and healing it, as well as your own body and soul. You must use it with confidence, knowing that it holds within it all that you will need. Know that I have packed it carefully. It is complete and tamper-free. As you use it, others will want what you have and you must share it with them freely—without fear and without reservation.

I am training a new generation of parents and grandparents to be equal to the times ahead. The babe I gave birth to is the living soul of the planet. That which you call Christ is the light at the heart of Life Itself, and that light must not be allowed to go out. I Myself will ensure that it endures on this planet. As its Mother, I will go to any lengths to protect what I have caused to be born into this world.

I invite you to join Me in the work of mothering—all males and females, the old and the young, the living as well as the dead. We are all one Mother of the world.

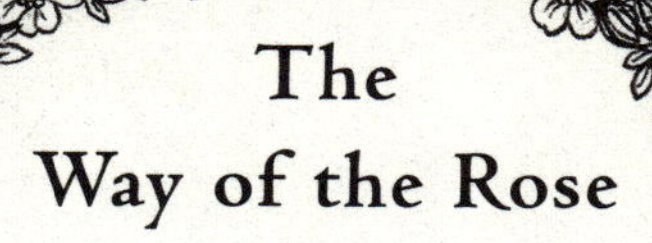

The Way of the Rose

WHEN WE COME TO THE END OF the rosary, only one thing remains to do—to crown the Lady with the garland of roses we have woven with our prayers. Those prayers aren't substitutes for the roses that our ancestors once used to crown their Queen. They *are* those roses. *We* are those roses. Seed to root, stem to flower, all living beings are bound together in one vast, interconnected body of prayer we call the Earth.

The oldest surviving species of rose today, from which all others are descended, is a French rose sometimes called *Rosa mundi*, or "Rose of the World." Still common, it was first cultivated in those parts of southern Europe where the earliest known statues of the Mother Goddess have been found. But roses are older than that. Roses are older than civilization. Older than human beings. Older even than hominids. Dig as deep as you can in the fossil record, and roses are there already. "In the beginning was the Word," says the Gospel of John. But the truth is, words came later. In the beginning was the Rose.

Appendix A

The Prayers of the Rosary

(Traditional Forms)

The Our Father

Our Father, Who art in heaven,
hallowed be Thy name;
Thy kingdom come; Thy will be done,
on earth as it is in heaven.
Give us this day our daily bread;
and forgive us our trespasses,
as we forgive those who trespass against us;
and lead us not into temptation,
but deliver us from evil. Amen.

The words of the traditional doxology, "For Thine is the Kingdom, the Power, and the Glory, forever and ever," were added to the Our Father by Protestant reformers. They are not included in the Catholic version that is recited in the rosary.

The Hail Mary

Hail Mary, full of grace, the Lord is with thee.
Blessed art thou amongst women,
and blessed is the fruit of thy womb, Jesus.
Holy Mary, Mother of God, pray for us sinners,
now and at the hour of our death. Amen.

Hidden in the familiar words of the Hail Mary is an ancient presence that the poet Robert Graves called the "Triple Goddess"— a female trinity of Maiden, Mother, and Crone.

The Maiden is the "Virgin" Mary when the angel arrives to say, "Hail Mary, full of grace, the Lord is with thee." The Mother is embodied in the words "Blessed art thou amongst women, and blessed is the fruit of thy womb, Jesus." The Crone is her aspect as Queen of the Dead: "Holy Mary, Mother of God, pray for us sinners, now and at the hour of our death."

The rhythm of the Hail Mary mantra naturally falls into these three parts, with a slight pause after each one. That female trinity, which both covers the powerful life cycle of every woman and embodies the full range of the Goddess's power, is inscribed within the Hail Mary as surely as if her triple image were carved there in stone.

The Glory Be

Glory be to the Father, and to the Son,
and to the Holy Spirit, as it was in the beginning,
is now, and ever shall be, world without end. Amen.

Additional Rosary Prayers

The Hail Holy Queen

Hail, Holy Queen, Mother of Mercy!
Hail our life, our sweetness, and our hope.
To thee do we cry, poor banished children of Eve:
to thee do we send up our sighs,
mourning and weeping in this valley of tears.
Turn then, most gracious Advocate,
thine eyes of mercy toward us,

and after this our exile, show unto us
the blessed fruit of thy womb, Jesus.
O clement, O loving, O sweet Virgin Mary!
Pray for us, Holy Mother of God,
that we may be worthy
of the promises of Christ. Amen.

The Memorare

Remember, O most gracious Virgin Mary,
that never was it known that anyone
who fled to thy protection, implored thy help,
or sought thine intercession was left unaided.
Inspired by this confidence, I fly to thee,
O Virgin of virgins, my Mother;
to thee do I come, before thee I stand,
sinful and sorrowful.
O Mother of the Word Incarnate,
despise not my petitions,
but in thy mercy hear and answer me. Amen.

The Fifteen Mysteries

The Joyful Mysteries

1. The Annunciation

The angel Gabriel appears to Mary and announces that, if she is willing, she may bring forth a child without a husband. In medieval art, Mary is often depicted illuminated by a shaft of sunlight, wearing over her red dress a robe of the deepest blue—the color of the ocean.

2. The Visitation

Now with child, Mary visits the home of her cousin Elizabeth, who, despite her advanced age, is also miraculously with child. The young woman and the old woman celebrate together the rising life force within them and its power to transform the world.

3. The Nativity

Mary gives birth in a cave used as a stable. In the darkness of the night, surrounded only by the animals, she brings her child into the world and lays him in a manger.

4. The Presentation

Mary presents her child to the greater community. On her way into the Temple, she encounters two ancient seers who recognize her as the Mother of God, but predict that a sword shall pierce her heart.

5. The Finding at the Temple

Mary loses her twelve-year-old son in Jerusalem. For three days she searches for him and eventually finds him discussing scripture with the elders in the Temple. Rather than leave him with these men, she brings him home to be with her.

The Sorrowful Mysteries

1. The Agony in the Garden

Jesus remains awake in the Garden of Gethsemane at night. The disciples have fallen asleep, unaware of the coming danger. Alone, he experiences the full weight of all the many sorrows to come.

2. The Scourging at the Pillar

Just as the land is furrowed by plows and the beasts are beaten into submission, the body of Mary's child is scourged. In the name of empire, Jesus is flogged by soldiers who are following the orders of their commanders.

3. The Crowning with Thorns

In the central mystery of the rosary, Jesus is mocked by those still fearful of the power he represents. He is given a red robe and a reed for a scepter—each an ancient symbol of the goddess. On his head is placed not a wreath of roses but a crown of thorns.

4. The Carrying of the Cross

A crowd gathers as Jesus is marched to his execution. No one intervenes. After Jesus stumbles and falls, a random onlooker who has come for the spectacle is forced by the soldiers to assume responsibility for carrying the cross.

5. The Crucifixion

The tree that once stood at the center of devotion to the Mother has been stripped of life and made an instrument of execution instead. When Jesus is dead, he is lowered into Mary's arms.

The Glorious Mysteries

1. The Resurrection

Following an ancient pattern whereby a slain god is resurrected by a mother or a lover, Mary Magdalene observes a sacred vigil at Jesus's tomb. On the third day, he appears to her at last. When she tells the other disciples, they refuse to believe her.

2. The Ascension

After his resurrection Jesus appears unexpectedly to various other disciples. On the fortieth day he disappears into a cloud, surrendering to the ceaseless cycle of birth, death, and rebirth that includes all life on Earth.

3. The Descent of the Holy Spirit

The disciples pray together with Mary for nine days after the Ascension. Finally, a mighty wind fills the room and the Holy Spirit descends upon them. The Hebrew word for spirit is *ruach*, which is feminine. In art, the Holy Spirit is often depicted as a dove—another sign of the Goddess.

4. The Assumption

Legend has it that Mary never dies but simply falls asleep and is "assumed" into heaven, her body and her spirit undivided. The body of the Great Mother is the body of the Earth and the body of the Heavens, the body of all that is.

5. The Coronation

In the final mystery of the rosary, Our Lady is crowned Queen of Heaven and Earth. Medieval statues of the Coronation showed Mary in the fullness of her power and glory, and yet mysteriously reborn and young again, holding the infant Christ. Life is a journey that circles back to where it started. This is where the rosary ends, and where it begins again.

Appendix B

A Way of the Rose Circle

The Way of the Rose is the path of the heart. We share that journey with pilgrims we meet on the way in a spirit of friendship and conversation. Our circles are open to men, women, and children and are free of dues or fees. We are not aligned with any existing religious organization or institution, nor are we concerned with building a new one. We come together to share our devotion to Our Lady, get our feet on the ground again, and find our way back to the garden of the Earth.

- We sit in a circle, and the only requirement for membership is a willingness to pray the rosary for our heart's desire and support others in doing the same.
- We begin each meeting by briefly sharing our stories—our experiences of prayer, of the mysteries, or of Our Lady—limiting each share to three minutes.
- We pray the rosary out loud together, reciting its words in unison. Individual members are invited to follow their conscience with regard to the precise wording of the prayers. This need not affect the overall harmonizing of the group's recitation.
- After the Hail Holy Queen, we take turns sharing our petitions for our heart's desires. As each person finishes praying, we recite a Hail Mary together.

- When the petitions are done, we invite the dead by name to join our circle—loved ones who have recently passed on, or those who have come to mind during the rosary. We then pray an additional "Decade for the Dead" of one Our Father, ten Hail Marys, and a Glory Be.
- At the conclusion of the Decade for the Dead, we stand, join hands, and recite the Memorare.
- At the close of each meeting, we make announcements and pass the hat, if necessary, to cover rent for our meeting space. Key holders and treasurers are service positions that rotate regularly. Our groups have no leaders, only spiritual friends.

Additional support can be found at wayoftherose.org or on our Way of the Rose Facebook group.

Acknowledgments

When Clark finished the manuscript for his previous book, *Waking Up to the Dark*, in the autumn of 2014, our friends were mostly skeptical about our prospects of getting such a radical, strange book into print. "Maybe you shouldn't mention the apparition," they'd say. "Couldn't you just stick to the memoir and environmental writing and . . . well, you know, maybe leave off that last part about the 'Girl'?" But the whole point of that book was to share Our Lady of Woodstock's "Gospel According to the Dark," and Clark and I were adamant that the record of the apparitions could not be altered or removed.

Still, we could see their point. Who would publish a book about a Marian apparition to an ex–Buddhist monk? Who would listen to a "Lady" who rarely referred to Jesus or even mentioned Catholicism, but had lots to say about climate change? Nevertheless, a few days after the manuscript was completed, Our Lady told Clark that the book would be published without significant alterations and that she had chosen the person to do it. "I will tell that person so in my own way." It would not be necessary for Clark to authenticate his experience by reporting it to the local Catholic bishop, as previous apparitionists had been required to do, but he would have to be willing to risk his career as a writer even so. "The editors are the bishops now," Our Lady explained. So that very night, Clark wrote letters to twenty of the top spiritual book editors in America and told them all of this. I prayed and tried my hardest not to panic as he pressed send.

One editor wrote back that, having read Our Lady's words, her life would never be the same—but there was no way she could publish such a book. Another, an old colleague of Clark's, wondered (only half in jest) if he was having some kind of breakdown. In the midst of all this, Our Lady gave Clark a vision of a tall, dark-haired woman reaching deep beneath the roots of a tree with a long, thin spade made of light. "Be prepared to meet with this woman in two weeks' time," she added. In his in-box the next morning was an email from the renowned editor Cindy Spiegel of Spiegel & Grau.

> *I'm 75% through, per my kindle, and I have to say I'm loving it. It's getting a bit weirder now, as you know, but I'm with you so far. I'm sorry it's taking so long—I find it hard to rush through. Let's speak when I'm done. It'll be soon. And in any case, I'd be delighted to meet with you. (In person with you or with her? I'd be delighted to meet with her, too.)*

Cindy offered to publish *Waking Up to the Dark* the following year without any significant changes, and soon afterward bought *The Way of the Rose* based on a brief proposal.

Throughout the daunting process of writing this book on the rosary, Cindy has been our collaborator and our guide. Her straightforward faith in Our Lady has offered both reassurance and validation, and her friendship and wide-ranging interests have enriched us at every turn. She knew when to give us all the time in the world . . . and when to take us out to lunch and ask the hard questions—questions it sometimes took months and months to answer. If *The Way of the Rose* finds a wide audience, it is thanks to her perseverance and her vision. Not only did Cindy help us craft our writing, but she guided us toward a deeper, wider understanding of the rosary itself.

As we hope we have shown, the rosary is a very old spiritual devotion with treelike roots reaching down through the millennia to the very depths of time. We are grateful and fortunate to have had a gardener whose "spade of light" could help us to illuminate its buried mysteries and recover its lost wisdom for a new generation of spiritual seekers.

Notes

Prologue

3 **But long before Mary, those same garlands:** Rose garlands were a customary offering for the Goddess throughout the ancient Mediterranean world, roses being associated with Venus, Aphrodite, Isis, and Inanna—to name only a few. A famous example can be found in Lucius Apuleius's second-century Latin novel *The Golden Ass*, in which the narrator drinks a potion that turns him into a donkey. It is only by consuming a rose garland woven for the goddess Isis that his human form can be restored. The entire novel is devoted to his quest to find such a garland—which, with Isis's help, he finally does. He becomes her lifelong devotee in the end. See *The Golden Ass*, trans. W. Adlington (Cambridge, MA: Harvard University Press, 1977).

4 **Old statues of Isis:** Ean Begg's book *The Cult of the Black Virgin* (London: Penguin Arkana, 1985) describes statues of Mary and Jesus that are virtually indistinguishable from Isis and Horus. Some are so old they may originally have been used in pagan worship. Made from stone or dark woods like ebony or walnut, these "Black Madonnas" are also aligned by their color with Isis, who was associated with the black soil of the Nile River delta.

4 **Buried in the soil:** Although Paleolithic goddess figurines have been unearthed all over the world, the highest concentration excavated to date come from those areas of Europe where the rosary first gained wide acceptance—especially Germany and southern France. The oldest figurines date from around 35,000 B.C.E.

5 **The most recent attempt to diminish:** For a thorough analysis of Mary's role in Catholicism following the reforms of Vatican II, see Charlene Spretnak's *Missing Mary: The Queen of Heaven and Her Reemergence in the Modern Church* (New York: Palgrave Macmillan, 2004).

6 **Throughout those years the Lady herself:** The late Catholic theologian Edward D. O'Connor addressed the dramatic rise in the number of Marian apparitions since 1830 in his book *Marian Apparitions Today: Why So Many?* (Santa Barbara, CA: Queenship Publishing, 1996).

7 **One of the most interesting speculations:** The American Zen poet and anthropologist Gary Snyder may have been the first to draw the connection between Paleolithic hunting behaviors and the focused attention of the modern meditator. In *Earth House Hold: Technical Notes & Queries to Fellow Dharma Revolutionaries* (New York: New Directions, 1969), he writes:

> The necessities of identity, intuition, stillness, that go with hunting make it seem as though shamanism and yoga and meditation may have their roots in the requirements of the hunter—where a man learns to be motionless for a day, putting his mind in an open state so that his consciousness won't spook creatures that he knows will be approaching.
>
> In spearfishing we learned you must never choose a specific fish for a quarry: you must let the fish choose you and be prepared to shoot the fish that will come into range (pp. 139–140).

Am I Not Here Who Am Your Mother?

14 **The tour began at a former Dominican convent:** Catholic tradition recognizes many manifestations of the Virgin Mary, each with her own special name. In the Litany of Loreto alone, for instance, she is addressed by fifty different titles, one of which is Our Lady of the Rosary.

That title refers to an apparition of Our Lady to St. Dominic in 1214. According to the fifteenth-century priest Alanus de Rupe, in that year Dominic was on a mission to convert the Cathars, a supposedly heretical Christian sect that had become popular in the Languedoc region of southern France and subsequently spread throughout Europe. When his mission ended in failure, Dominic retreated to the woods near Toulouse, where he prayed and fasted in a cave.

After several days, the Virgin Mary appeared. She fed Dominic milk from her breast to restore his strength and then told him that his method of conversion was the wrong one to use with the Cathars. Rather than the "battering ram" of fiery sermons, he should use the gentler method of her Angelic Psalter (the rosary), which she then taught him how to pray. Dominic followed her guidance, and the Cathars, who had previously resisted all efforts to bring them back into the Catholic fold, were converted through the rosary.

This story was accepted as historical fact until the late nineteenth century, when it was discovered that Alanus de Rupe had invented it to legitimize his claim that the rosary had originated in his own Dominican order. In reality, Dominic never prayed the rosary, and he failed utterly in his efforts to convert the Cathars. They were exterminated by the Catholic Church a few years later in a campaign so ruthless and well organized that Hitler used it as his model for the Holocaust. In one day alone, twenty thousand men, women, and children were slaughtered with the blessing of the ironically named Pope Innocent III.

For an older, more historically grounded legend on the origin of the rosary, see the chapter beginning on page 55 entitled "Flowers Become Prayers." For an account of Alanus de Rupe and his role in spreading the Dominican version, refer to Herbert Thurston's article "Alan de Rupe and His Indulgence of 60,000 Years," in *The Month*, no. 459 (September 1902), pp. 281–299.

17 **"She's the Catholic version":** In Europe and the Mediterranean, the Catholic Church went to great lengths to deny any connection between the Virgin Mary and the Magna Mater (Great Mother) of the pagan world. It adopted a different tactic in the New World. Throughout the Americas, the Church followed a syncretic approach, whereby it allowed the figure of the Virgin to be "grafted" onto figures such as Pachamama (the Andean goddess of fertility) and Tonantzin (the earth goddess of the Aztecs). To the Church, this was an expedient strategy to aid their efforts at mass conversion. There is no evidence that any Catholic authority believed what the indigenous people of the sixteenth-century Americas clearly understood to be true—that these goddesses and the Virgin Mary were one and the same.

18 **Later that afternoon, I found a book:** Originally written in Nahuatl, the language of the Aztecs, the *Nican Mopohua* preserves the traditional account of the Guadalupe apparitions. Many English translations can be found, some with extensive commentary. The strangest, most speculative of these is John Mini's *The Aztec Virgin: The Secret Mystical Tradition of Our Lady of Guadalupe* (Sausalito, CA: Trans-Hyperborean Institute of Science, 2000). The most tragic (in every sense) is *Guadalupe: Mother of the New Creation* (Maryknoll, NY: Orbis Books, 1997), written by a Mexican American priest regarded as "the father of U.S. Latino religious thought." A leading figure in the

Liberation Theology Movement, Virgil Elizondo took his own life in 2016 following accusations of child molestation.

19 **The Virgin of Guadalupe appeared:** In *Guadalupe: Mother of the New Creation*, Virgil Elizondo recounts the horrors of the Mesoamerican genocide from the point of view of a modern Mexican American who is also a Catholic priest, reflecting upon the tragic past of his ancestors from that dual perspective (see previous note). For a firsthand account of the atrocities committed by the Spanish against the indigenous peoples of the Americas, see "A Short Account of the Destruction of the Indies," written by the Dominican friar Bartolomé de las Casas in 1542. For a modern treatment of the same, see Jarod Diamond's *Guns, Germs, and Steel: The Fates of Human Societies* (New York: Norton, 1997).

19 **What happened to the natural world:** For a comprehensive account of ecological depredation in early colonial America, and a lyrical eulogy for all that has been lost, consult *Paradise Found: Nature in America at the Time of Discovery* (Chicago: University of Chicago Press, 2009), by Steve Nicholls.

22 **I discovered that as far back:** John D. Miller offers the best overview of bead practices across multiple religious traditions. His book *Beads & Prayers: The Rosary in History & Devotion* (London: Burns & Oates, 2002) contains a useful diagram titled "The Evolution of the Marian Rosary" and an extensive "Chronology of the Development of the Rosary" from 1750 B.C.E. to the present.

23 **Current projections tell us:** In his book *Half-Earth: Our Planet's Fight for Life* (New York: Liveright, 2016), the American environmental biologist E. O. Wilson writes, "Unless humanity learns a great deal more about global biodiversity, and moves quickly to protect it, we will soon lose most of the species composing life on Earth" (see p. 3). Only one year later, on July 25, 2017, the journal *Proceedings of the National Academy of Sciences* published a comprehensive study concluding with words of warning that the authors themselves seemed to believe would never be heeded: "We emphasize that the sixth mass extinction is already here and the window for effective action is very short, probably two or three decades at most. All signs point to ever more powerful assaults on biodiversity in the next two decades, painting a dismal picture of the future of life, including human life." See "Biological Annihilation via the Ongoing Sixth Mass Extinction Signaled by Vertebrate Population Losses and Declines," by Gerardo Ceballos, Paul R. Ehrlich, and Rodolfo Dirzo.

Mother

26 **These first goddesses were endlessly varied:** For a seminal treatment of goddess figurines and their significance for peoples of the Upper Paleolithic, see *Civilization of the Goddess: The World of Old Europe* (HarperSanFrancisco, 1991), by Marija Gimbutas. It is worth noting that only goddess figurines come down to us from the period immediately preceding the Neolithic era. No male gods have been found.

Mantra

28 **That is why some modern scholars:** In *Ritual and Mantras: Rules Without Meaning* (New York: North-Holland, 1986), the Vedic scholar Frits Staal suggests that mantras, because they are tied to rituals that predate the development of human language, might be compared to birdsongs in their musicality, the precision of their rhythms, and their extreme antiquity.

Mystery

31 **In the Gospel of Luke, Mary tells her cousin:** Because it begins with the words "My soul doth magnify the Lord," Mary's extemporaneous speech in the first chapter of Luke became known as the Magnificat. Its central verses read like a revolutionary manifesto:

He [the Lord] has performed mighty deeds with his arm;
he has scattered those who are proud in their inmost thoughts.
He has brought down rulers from their thrones
but has lifted up the humble.
He has filled the hungry with good things
but has sent the rich away empty. (Luke 1:51–53)

32 **The rosary rejects the fiery apocalypse:** Regarding the replacement of the Last Judgment with the Coronation of Mary as the final mystery of the rosary, Anne Winston-Allen concludes: "Most people preferred the happier ending because they hoped for clemency from Mary rather than for justice." See *Stories of the Rose: The Making of the Rosary in the Middle Ages* (University Park: Pennsylvania State University Press, 1997).

32 **In the mystery religions:** The mystery cults of the ancient world arose in agricultural societies that were deeply rooted in the rhythms of the natural world. The most influential of these were the mysteries of Isis and Osiris, which originated in Egypt and later spread throughout the Roman Empire, and the Eleusinian Mysteries, which took the stories of the Greek grain goddess Demeter and her daughter Persephone (also called Kore, "the Maiden") as their subject. The mysteries were revealed to devotees during a series of seasonal initiations tied to agricultural festivals and were not to be shared with outsiders.

Interest in the mystery religions of the ancient world became widespread during the late nineteenth century following the publication of *The Golden Bough,* by the Scottish anthropologist James George Frazer. Frazer ignited controversy among the Christian faithful by insisting that—with its story of birth, death, and renewal (resurrection)—Christianity itself was a mystery religion and was therefore essentially a carryover from the pagan beliefs and rituals of earlier times. Today, the older mystery religion that lies at the heart of Christianity can still be found in the fifteen episodes from the lives of Mary and Jesus that compose the rosary—episodes that, not coincidentally, are referred to as "mysteries."

For those wishing to read Frazer's magnum opus of early anthropology, we recommend this one-volume edition: *The Golden Bough: A Study in Magic and Religion* (Oxford: Oxford University Press, 1994). This version restores controversial writings on the crucifixion and resurrection of Jesus that were suppressed in many earlier editions.

How to Pray the Rosary

35 **Medieval people made their own rosaries:** Not surprisingly, the best book on medieval rosaries was written by a member of the Society for Creative Anachronism, an international nonprofit organization devoted to researching and re-creating the arts and skills of pre-seventeenth-century Europe. Chris Laning's *Bedes Byddyng: Medieval Rosaries & Paternoster Beads* (Milpitas, CA: Society for Creative Anachronism, 2007) remains the best single source of information on the structure and material composition of the medieval rosary. For further access to her vast reservoir of knowledge on this subject, visit her websites: http://paternoster-row.medievalscotland.org/ and https://paternosters.blogspot.com/.

35 **"Choose whichever method pleases you":** Arguably the most influential and widely read manual on the Catholic rosary, *The Secret of the Rosary*, written by St. Louis de Montfort (1673–1716), is available online and in numerous print editions. Although de Montfort's writings reflect the pious Catholic beliefs and sentiments of his day, his approach to the rosary is practical, generous, and forgiving, lacking the rigidity of later Catholic manuals on the subject. The book is divided into fifty-three chapters called "Roses"—one for each Hail Mary of the rosary. *The Way of the Rose* takes the same approach, adding six additional chapters for the Our Father beads, for a total of fifty-nine.

It's All Downhill from Here

48 **When he marched through the Bible:** For a book-length treatment of the "koans of the Bible," see *How to Believe in God: Whether You Believe in Religion or Not* (New York: Doubleday, 2008), by Clark Strand.

48 **He researched an emerging branch of Buddhism:** To learn about the Soka Gakkai International, consult *Waking the Buddha: How the Most Dynamic and Empowering Buddhist Movement in History Is Changing Our Concept of Religion* (Santa Monica, CA: Middleway Press, 2014), by Clark Strand.

49 **In 2009, the president's chief science adviser:** Twice, in an April 8, 2009, interview with the Associated Press, chief White House science adviser John Holdren used this metaphor to describe the impending catastrophe of global warming: "We're driving in a car with bad brakes in a fog and headed for a cliff. We know for sure that cliff is out there. We just don't know exactly where it is."

49 **But what did "recovery from excess" really mean?:** A 2011 article uses the language of Alcoholics Anonymous to explore our collective relationship to ecological crisis:

> What will restore us to sanity? What "Power greater than ourselves" is capable of steering an out-of-control species back on course for its journey through deep time? The answer is the planet, of course. God relieved A.A. founder Bill W. of his compulsion to drink, and since that initial recovery countless others have been saved from the heartbreak of all kinds of addictions in virtually every country around the globe—by Buddha, by Allah,

> by Avalokiteshvara, by Vishnu, by Nature, and by a plurality of other sanity-producing "Higher Powers"—but only the globe itself is big enough to cure a species. Where else can it turn for guidance and inspiration but to the mother who birthed it from the depths of her evolutionary womb?

From "Restored to Sanity," by Clark Strand (*Tricycle: The Buddhist Review*, Spring 2011).

51 **Then the round, moonlike face:** For a complete account of the initial apparitions of Our Lady of Woodstock, see "Part III: The Black Madonna" in *Waking Up to the Dark: Ancient Wisdom for a Sleepless Age*, by Clark Strand (New York: Spiegel & Grau, 2015).

51 **I was ghostwriting a book:** See *The Reluctant Psychic: A Memoir*, by Suzan Saxman with Perdita Finn (New York: St. Martin's Press, 2015).

53 **When the apparition ended:** For the full text see *Waking Up to the Dark*, "Part IV: Gospel According to the Dark."

Flowers Become Prayers

55 **Once there was a young boy:** Interesting variations on this story can be found in *The Franciscan Crown*, by Marion A. Habig (New York: Franciscan Herald Press, 1976); *Stories of the Rose*, by Anne Winston-Allen; and *The Rose-Garden Game: A Tradition of Beads and Flowers*, by Eithne Wilkins (New York: Herder and Herder, 1969). *Stories of the Rose* includes a wood-block illustration from an early-sixteenth-century rosary confraternity manual in which the Lady withdraws roses from a kneeling monk's mouth as he prays.

The Name of the Rose

58 **She has been known by many names:** For an exhaustive treatment of the Goddess in her myriad forms throughout Western civilization, see *The Myth of the Goddess: Evolution of an Image*, by Jungian analysts Anne Baring and Jules Cashford (London: Penguin Arkana, 1991). More than a quarter century after its initial publication, this book remains an indispensable resource on the subject. For a broader approach, including detailed descriptions and images of goddesses from cultures around the world, see Hallie Iglehart Austen's *The Heart of the Goddess: Art, Myth and Meditations of the World's Sacred Feminine* (Rhinebeck, NY: Monkfish Publishing, 2018).

58 **In 1858, the fourteen-year-old French peasant:** The apparitions of Our Lady of Lourdes have been the subject of numerous books, novels, and films. The best novel remains *The Song of Bernadette*, by Franz Werfel (New York: Viking, 1942). A prominent Jewish intellectual and an outspoken critic of Hitler, Werfel was forced in 1938 to flee Austria for France, where he and his wife were sheltered by the people of Lourdes. While there he learned about the apparitions and made a vow that, if he escaped to America, he would write a novel about Bernadette. Werfel kept this promise, and the result was an instant bestseller. The book is divided into five sections, each consisting of ten chapters. The final chapter is called "The Fiftieth Ave," making it clear that Werfel intended for the novel to mirror the structure of the rosary. The best nonfiction book on Bernadette and the Lourdes apparitions is *Bernadette Speaks: A Life of Saint Bernadette Soubirous in Her Own Words*, by René Laurentin (Boston: Pauline Books & Media, 2000). Laurentin's account offers the most detailed and accurate treatment of the saint's life and includes many photographs.

59 **Moses asks, "Who are you?":** For a chapter-length discussion of Moses's encounter with Yahweh at the burning bush, see "The Name of God" in *How to Believe in God: Whether You Believe in Religion or Not*, by Clark Strand.

Is Mary Real?

61 **Dirt is what happens when life happens:** *Dirt: The Ecstatic Skin of the Earth*, by William Bryant Logan (New York: Norton, 1995), offers a lyrical but scientifically rigorous history of soil, from its origins on the planet down to the present day.

61 **Month after month, she will vanish:** For an encyclopedic tour of moon myths, symbols, and legends, see Jules Cashford's *The Moon: Myth and Image* (New York: Four Walls Eight Windows, 2003). For a feminist treatment of the moon cycle in myth and astrology, consult *Mysteries of the Dark Moon: The Healing Power of the Dark Goddess*, by Demetra George (New York: HarperOne, 1992).

Our Lady of Rocamadour

63 **During a two-year period:** There are roughly 300 Black Virgins in Europe, 150 of which are found in France. Among these, Our Lady of Rocamadour is one of the most famous. Between 1172 and 1173, a

scribe sat at the entrance to her cliffside chapel in south-central France recording the stories of pilgrims, some of whom had traveled over a thousand miles to reach her—to ask for a miracle, or to offer thanks when a miracle had been granted. These were collected under the title *The Miracles of Our Lady of Rocamadour* and account for some of the best-known stories of the Middle Ages. For an English version of the complete stories, see *The Miracles of Our Lady of Rocamadour: Analysis and Translation*, by Marcus Bull (Woodbridge, UK: Boydell Press, 1999).

Moses vs. Mama

68 **In the oral legends that preceded Moses:** In *The Myth of the Goddess*, Anne Baring and Jules Cashford write: "In every major archaeological excavation in Palestine female figures have been found, dating to between 2000 BC and 600 BC. Women may have used these tiny images to appeal to Asherah to help them in childbirth or to grant them fertility" (p. 456). Asherah was associated with trees and was worshipped as the Giver of Life. A prolonged war was waged upon her devotees by later Jewish prophets, although her statue once occupied the Temple at Jerusalem.

69 **He named the boy Rahula:** For an extended reflection on the place of family and children in Buddhism, see "What Name Did the Buddha Give His Son?" by Clark Strand (*Tricycle: The Buddhist Review*, Summer 2002).

Scene of the Crime

71 **Yet we can also read the Bible's version:** The comparison is well known among scholars of Semitic and Babylonian literature. Baring and Cashford summarize the influence of the earlier story in *The Myth of the Goddess*:

> The Enuma Elish is the first story of the replacing of a mother goddess who generates creation as part of herself by a god who "makes" creation as something separate from himself. All myths of the Iron Age in which a sky or sun god or hero conquers a great serpent or dragon can be traced to this Babylonian epic . . . Its influence can be followed through Hittite, Assyrian, Persian, Canaanite, Hebrew, Greek, and Roman mythology (see p. 273).

72 **The decision to see our Mother:** It is worth noting that this idea remains foundational for Western culture. In his bestselling book *12 Rules for Life: An Antidote to Chaos* (Toronto: Random House Canada, 2018), the antifeminist Canadian psychologist Jordan Peterson describes Tiamat not as the "Great" Mother of early Mesopotamian religion, but as the archetypal "Terrible" Mother:

> The Terrible Mother is the spirit of careless unconsciousness, tempting the ever-striving spirit of awareness and enlightenment down into the protective womb-like embrace of the underworld. It's the terror young men feel towards attractive women, who are nature itself, ever ready to reject them, intimately, at the deepest possible level. Nothing inspires self-consciousness, undermines courage, and fosters feelings of nihilism and hatred more than that—except, perhaps, the too-tight embrace of too-caring mom (pp. 323–324).

Caring mothers are bad. Attractive women are bad. Even wombs are bad. Nature herself is a force of chaos that must be set in order, just as women must be dominated by men.

72 **Humans had art, dance, music, storytelling:** Christine Desdemaines-Hugon makes a compelling case for the sudden flowering of human culture during the Upper Paleolithic in her book, *Stepping-Stones: A Journey Through the Ice Age Caves of the Dordogne* (New Haven: Yale University Press, 2012).

73 **For tens of thousands of years:** For a comprehensive look at the relationship between the Goddess and her snake allies from Paleolithic to classical times, see "Part Four: The Serpent" in Buffie Johnson's *Lady of the Beasts: Ancient Images of the Goddess and Her Sacred Animals* (San Francisco: HarperSanFrancisco, 1988).

Life Goes in a Circle

76 **Life is a circle to which nothing:** In its June 16, 1972, report for the Stockholm Conference, convened by the United Nations to address the looming environmental catastrophes of the twentieth and twenty-first centuries, the Friends of the Earth wrote:

> Life holds to one central truth: that all matter and energy needed for life moves in great closed circles from which nothing escapes

> and to which only the driving fire of the sun is added. Life devours itself: everything that eats is itself eaten; every chemical that is made by life can be broken down by life; all the sunlight that can be used is used. Of all that there is on earth, nothing is taken away by life, and nothing is added by life—but nearly everything is used by life, used and reused in thousands of complex ways, moved through vast chains of plants and animals and back again to the beginning.

The complete text of the report can be found in *The Stockholm Conference: Only One Earth* (London: Earth Island Limited, 1972). An excerpted version is anthologized in *American Earth: Environmental Writing Since Thoreau*, edited by Bill McKibben (New York: Library of America, 2008).

The Reenchantment of the World

78 **The rosary is a prayer well suited:** *Waking Up to the Dark: Ancient Wisdom for a Sleepless Age*, by Clark Strand, offers a book-length exploration of nighttime prayer rituals and spiritual practices other than the rosary.

Made for Each Other

80 **What is it about roses:** Published in *Spiritus: A Journal of Christian Spirituality* (vol. 4, no. 1, Spring 2004), Rachel Fulton's essay "The Virgin in the Garden, or Why Flowers Make Better Prayers" offers a convincing answer to this question. In that article, Fulton combines her knowledge of medieval Marian devotions with the aesthetic theory of Elaine Scarry and the paleobotany of Michael Pollan as set forth in his book *The Botany of Desire: A Plant's-Eye View of the World* (New York: Random House, 2002). The essay concludes:

> Flowers partake of our flesh; indeed, as we have seen, they are in a very real sense the source of our flesh. They also, in ways that we are only just beginning to understand, partake of our minds—and so of our affects and attention. They are keyed not only to our memories, but also to the faculties of our imagination. In them we see a beauty that is at once other—a plant, not an

animal—and a reflection of ourselves. We plant them in gardens, but they respond only insofar as cultivation answers their own needs. If they need us, it is because we need them. Why, in the end, do they make better prayers? Because prayer is a work both of the imagination—holding the image of the beloved steady in one's mind—and of the flesh, as we know whenever we hold an object such as a string of beads or a flower in our hands and find ourselves better able to concentrate. I will leave it to you what it is that the Beloved sees.

The Broken Rosary

85 **I knew that the usual protocol in cases:** In 1978, in response to a century that saw four times as many Marian apparitions as the century before, the Sacred Congregation for the Doctrine of the Faith issued a set of guidelines to formalize the manner in which the Catholic Church responded to such apparitions. These began with the local bishop, who, after conducting an investigation, could declare the apparition worthy of belief by the Catholic faithful or discount it altogether—or, in the event that the results were inconclusive, pass the matter up the chain of command to the national bishops' conference of his country, or even to the pope. For the statistics on modern apparitions, visit the website of the University of Dayton's International Marian Research Institute: https://udayton.edu/imri/mary/a/apparitions-statistics-modern.php

A summary from that site explaining the frequency of Marian apparitions in the twentieth century and the Catholic Church's response to them includes the following:

> A statistical analysis of the Marian apparition directory reveals the following results. During the twentieth century, there have been 386 cases of Marian apparitions. The Church has made "no decision" about the supernatural character regarding 299 of the 386 cases. The Church has made a "negative decision" about the supernatural character in seventy-nine of the 386 cases. Out of the 386 apparitions, the Church has decided that "yes" there is a supernatural character only in eight cases: Fatima (Portugal), Beauraing (Belgium), Banneux (Belgium), Akita (Japan), Syracuse (Italy), Zeitoun (Egypt), Manila (Philippines) (according to

some sources), and Betania (Venezuela). Local bishops have approved of the faith expression at the sites where these eight apparitions occurred. Besides the eight approved apparitions, there have been eleven (out of the 386 apparitions) which have not been approved with a "supernatural character," but which have received a "yes" to indicate the local bishop's "approval of faith expression (prayer and devotion) at the site."

85 **That she'd called for the return of the forests:** For Our Lady's words on these subjects, see "Part IV: Gospel According to the Dark" in Clark Strand's *Waking Up to the Dark*.

90 **Q: Is the use of the rosary a universal request:** See *Queen of the Cosmos: Interviews with the Visionaries of Medjugorje*, by Janice T. Connell (Orleans, MA: Paraclete Press, 1992), p. 113. Another interview with the same visionary, Marija Pavlovic, contains the following exchange:

Q: "Is the message [of Our Lady of Medjugorje] for Hindus and Buddhists, for Jews and Protestants, Moslems and atheists?"

A: "Yes. The message is for everyone who wants to live!" (p. 106)

92 **Later, in a book called:** For the graph in question, see *Marian Apparitions Today: Why So Many?*, p. 76.

Wild at Heart

97 **Nature doesn't care much for grates or gates:** The beauty, tenacity, and extraordinary resilience of the natural world is the theme of Alan Weisman's brilliant work of speculative ecology *The World Without Us* (New York: St. Martin's Press, 2007). Weisman explains how the massive infrastructure that allows for our modern lives must be constantly defended against natural forces that, in the absence of human beings, would quickly disassemble it and reclaim it for the soil.

Sex, Death, and Roses

100 **Apart from its literal use:** Anne Winston-Allen's *Stories of the Rose* includes an entire chapter on rose gardens and their relation to the rosary and, more broadly, to Marian symbolism. See "Chapter 4: Secular Love Gardens, Marian Iconography, and the Names of the Rose."

101 **This becomes understandable when we consider:** A regrettable but by no means unusual example of religious misogyny is to be found in the *Theragāthā,* a collection of poems attributed to the earliest Buddhist monks:

> You little hut made of a chain of bones, sewn together with
> flesh and sinew.
> Fie upon the evil-smelling body. You cherish those who have
> another's limbs.
> You bag of dung, tied up with skin, you demoness with lumps
> on your breast.
> There are nine streams in your body which flow all the time.
> Your body with its nine streams makes an evil smell and is obstructed by dung.
> A bhikkhu [male monastic] desiring purity avoids it as one
> avoids excrement.
> If any person knew you as I know you, he would avoid you,
> keeping
> far away, as one avoids a cess-pit in the rainy season.

See *The Elders' Verses. Vol. I: Theragāthā* (London: Pali Text Society, 1969), translated by Kenneth R. Norman, verses 1146–1208.

How Much Is Enough?

103 **As much as they could carry:** In *A History of the World in 100 Objects* (New York: Viking, 2010), British Museum Director Neil MacGregor writes:

> What do you take with you when you travel? Most of us would embark on a long list that begins with a toothbrush and ends with excess baggage. But for most of human history, there was only one thing that you really needed in order to travel—a stone handaxe. A handaxe was the Swiss Army knife of the Stone Age, an essential piece of technology with multiple uses. The pointed end could be used as a drill, while the long blades on either side would cut trees or meat or scrape bark or skins. It looks pretty straightforward, but in fact the handaxe is extremely tricky to make and, for more than a million years, it was literally the cut-

ting edge of technology. It accompanied our ancestors through half of their history, enabling them to spread first across Africa and then across the world. (p. 15)

104 **The Neolithic Revolution brought us war:** Since 1950 many books and scholarly articles have been published chronicling the transition from the hunter-gatherer societies of the Upper Paleolithic to the agricultural city-states that developed during the Neolithic. However, one of the most accessible overviews of that transition and its implications for today is to be found in a novel. Daniel Quinn tried several nonfiction approaches to a book exposing the lie of human supremacy, which he called "the most dangerous idea in existence," before writing *Ishmael: An Adventure of the Mind and Spirit* (New York: Bantam, 1992). In that novel, the narrator becomes the disciple of a talking gorilla, who guides him through an alternative (nonhuman) reading of human history, including a radical reinterpretation of biblical myths and stories.

Rosary Alchemy

107 **By murmuring the prayers of the rosary:** With its repetitive pattern of one Our Father and ten Hail Marys, the rosary remains, at bottom, a celebration of the *Hieros Gamos*, or "Sacred Marriage"—a sexual ritual preserved in ancient pagan art and, in the Bible, in the erotic love poetry of the Song of Songs. That ritual reenacted the divine union between a god and goddess, mirroring the creative forces of nature. In medieval alchemy the *Hieros Gamos* took the form of a "chemical marriage" between Luna (the Moon) and Sol (the Sun).

Virtually every modern Catholic writer on the rosary minimizes or completely ignores its profound connection to alchemy. And yet, medieval alchemical texts are replete with images drawn from the mysteries of the rosary, including direct references to the Annunciation, Resurrection, Ascension, Descent of the Holy Spirit, Assumption, and Coronation of Mary as Queen of Heaven and Earth. One of the most famous picture allegories features the courtship, sexual union, and divine marriage of Sol and Luna. Its name? *Rosarium Philosophorum*, or "The Rosary of the Philosophers."

For a detailed explanation of the Sacred Marriage, see the chapter "The Hidden Goddess in the Old Testament" in *The Myth of the God-*

dess, pages 479–485. For illustrations from various versions of the *Rosarium Philosophorum*, see *Alchemy & Mysticism* (Cologne: Taschen, 2018), by Alexander Roob.

Are You the Gardener?

109 **In ancient Egyptian legends:** The excavation of the "sunken" Egyptian cities of Thonis-Heracleion and Canopus by French archaeologist Franck Goddio in 2000 has opened a vast reservoir of knowledge about the ancient seasonal rites associated with Isis and Osiris. Along with the many statues, stiles, sarcophagi, vases, lamps, and ritual religious objects that Goddio recovered is a vat intended for use in the "Garden Mysteries" of Isis and Osiris. Into this container an effigy of Osiris would have been placed during a yearly festival. A "widow" playing the role of Isis would pour a mixture of river silt and barley into the effigy, and to this mixture water would be added so that the seeds would germinate, symbolically renewing the land. For more information, see *Osiris: Egypt's Sunken Mysteries*, by Franck Goddio and David Fabre (Paris: Flammarion, 2015).

109 **In early Sumerian hymns:** These can be found in *Inanna, Queen of Heaven and Earth: Her Stories and Hymns from Sumer*, by Diane Wolkstein and Samuel Noah Kramer (New York: Harper & Row, 1983). Sexuality is explicitly linked to the fertility of the land in these poems and hymns, and there is no evidence of negative attitudes toward the body. Rather, they revel in its pleasures, its beauty, and its fecundity.

In *The Courtship of Inanna and Dumuzi*, for instance, Dumuzi's phallus is compared to a cloud-soaring grove:

At the king's lap stood the rising cedar.
Plants grew high by their side.
Grains grew high by their side.
Gardens flourished luxuriantly. (p.37)

A few verses later Inanna says of her lover:

He brought me into his garden.
My brother Dumuzi brought me into his garden . . .
Before my lord Dumuzi,
I poured out plants from my womb. (p. 40)

110 **In fact, the word *virgin* meant:** The English writer Marina Warner devotes an entire chapter to the Virgin birth in her feminist masterpiece *Alone of All Her Sex: The Myth and the Cult of the Virgin Mary* (New York: Vintage, 1983). Noting that the word used to refer to Mary as a virgin in the New Testament is *parthenos*, a Greek term with its own set of associations, none of which pertain to chastity, she writes:

> In the case of pagan goddesses, the sign of the virgin rarely endorses chastity as a virtue. Venus, Ishtar, Astarte, and Anat, the love goddesses of the near east and classical mythology, are entitled virgin despite their lovers, who die and rise again for them each year . . . their sacred virginity symbolized their autonomy, and had little or no moral connotation. They spurned men because they were preeminent, independent, and alone, which is why the title virgin could be used of a goddess who entertained lovers. Her virginity signified she had retained freedom of choice: to take lovers or to reject them (pp. 47–48).

Woven Together as One

120 **In sacred art, the Virgin:** A spindle is a long spike, often weighted with a disc or "whorl" to steady its circular movement in spinning yarn by hand. Spindle whorls have been found in women's graves from Neolithic times, suggesting that their owners were closely identified with the work of spinning and the ancient symbolism associated with that task. In *The Rose-Garden Game*, Eithne Wilkins writes:

> Like that other archaic and fundamental skill, the smith's, spinning is a magical art. Briar Rose's enchantment [in Sleeping Beauty], for instance, is caused by pricking her finger on a spindle; and as one "spins a yarn," so one "weaves" a spell. Whether in Greek, Germanic, Mayan, or other myth, the Fates are always spinners and weavers, the archaic female triad outside of space and time, more potent than any society of gods, and the Great Mother herself spins and weaves because she is the primal embodiment of the triad of the weavers of all things earthly, of growth, of time, of destiny. The primordial Lady spins, out of her own being, the thread of time and weaves it to make the tissue of things, just as the woman spins in herself the tissue of another being's flesh . . . Spinning and weaving are occupations, then,

proper to the Virgin Mary as the Great Mother, and it is probably not accidental that two parts of the spinning-wheel machinery are called "the maiden" and "mother-of-all," or that the number 15 plays a significant part both in spinstress-lore and in the rosary (pp. 96–97).

For an account of Mary spinning yarn for the Temple veil, read "The Proto-Gospel of James," in Bart D. Ehrman's *Lost Scriptures: Books That Did Not Make It into the New Testament* (Oxford: Oxford University Press, 2003).

The Lost Language of Prayer

125 **The anthropologist Claude Lévi-Strauss:** See "Chapter 2: 'Primitive' Thinking and the 'Civilized' Mind" in *Myth and Meaning: Cracking the Code of Culture,* by Claude Lévi-Strauss (New York: Schocken, 1979).

127 **a 12-step look at "cultural addiction":** Albert J. LaChance's book *Cultural Addiction: The Greenspirit Guide to Recovery* (Berkeley, CA: North Atlantic Books, 1991) was the first book-length work to attempt an AA-style approach to recovery from modern consumerism and resource depletion.

What If I Don't Get It Right?

140 **A surprising example of that kind of avoidance:** The relevant portion of *Nican Mopohua,* the Nahuatl account of the apparitions, reads:

> That Tuesday, when it was still very dark, Juan Diego left his home to call a priest at Tlatilcolo. And when he drew near the side of the little hill at the base of the mountain range where the road comes, on the side where the sun sets, where he would normally go, he said: "If I go straight along the road, the Lady may catch sight of me, for it is certain that, as before, she will stop me to take the sign to the Bishop as she ordered me . . ."
>
> At once he took a turn around the hill, climbed up the middle, crossing toward the east side in order to arrive quickly in Mexico [City], so that the Queen of Heaven would not stop him. He thought that because of the way he took she would not see him, she who sees perfectly everywhere. Then he spotted her

coming down over the hill. She had been watching him from where she had first seen him.

She came to meet him on the other side of the hill, intercepted him, and asked: "What is happening, smallest of my sons? Where are you going, where are you heading?" And, perhaps because he was embarrassed or ashamed or perhaps scared or frightened in her presence, he fell to his knees, greeted her and said: "My young Lady, my tiniest Daughter, my little Girl . . . It is with sorrow that I bring anguish to your face, your heart: I want you to know, my little Girl, that my uncle your servant is gravely ill . . . Forgive me, I beg you, and be patient with me for now; for I will not mislead you, my youngest Daughter, my little Girl. Tomorrow, without fail, I will come in all haste."

As soon as she had heard Juan Diego's arguments she, the faithful perfect Virgin, answered: "Hear me, my youngest son, and hold it fast in your heart that there is nothing to be afraid of or to make you anxious. Let not your face or heart be troubled. Be not afraid of this illness, or of any other sickness or painful affliction. Am I not here, I your Mother?"

See *The Theological Message of Guadalupe,* by Salvador Carrillo Alday (New York: Society of St. Paul/Alba House, 2010), verses 99–119.

No One Gets Left Out

143 **According to one medieval legend:** This version of the story has been adapted from *The Miracles of Our Lady Saint Mary: Brought Out of Diverse Tongues and Newly Set Forth in English,* by Evelyn Underhill (New York: Dutton, 1906).

Pass It On

146 **Fellowships called "confraternities":** Although these fellowships have been discussed by numerous religious scholars, Anne Winston-Allen offers the most thoughtful analysis of their role in spreading the rosary. See Chapter 3 of *Stories of the Rose.*

146 **Perhaps the closest equivalent we have now:** For more on AA group culture and its nonhierarchical rules of self-governance, see the book *Alcoholics Anonymous: The Story of How Many Thousands of Men and*

Women Have Recovered from Alcoholism, 4th ed. (New York: Alcoholics Anonymous World Services, 2001).

147 **Ernest Kurtz traced the rapid spread:** See *Not-God: A History of Alcoholics Anonymous*, by Ernest Kurtz (Center City, MN: Hazelden, 1979).

The Human Agenda

149 **Both view human beings as the pinnacle:** For books on anthropocentrism and its consequences for the natural world, consult *After Eden: The Evolution of Human Domination*, by Kirkpatrick Sale (Durham, NC: Duke University Press, 2006), and *The Myth of Human Supremacy*, by Derrick Jensen (New York: Seven Stories Press, 2016).

Our Lady of the Beasts

151 **Some of the earliest statues:** See *Lady of the Beasts*, by Buffie Johnson.

151 **All beings in the natural world:** Bernd Heinrich's *Life Everlasting: The Animal Way of Death* (New York: Houghton Mifflin Harcourt, 2012) offers nonfiction science writing at its very best. The opening chapter alone—about an undertaker beetle burying a mouse and finding a mate—is enough to awaken most readers to the extraordinary commingling of joy and sorrow in the natural world.

The Dead Are Right Here

156 **While traditional rosaries have five decades:** Information about the rosary that was once called the *Corone* (or "Crown") of Our Lady is notoriously hard to come by. Although this form of the rosary was once as popular as the five-decade rosary (even more popular in Rome, it seems), it is now virtually extinct. Six-decade rosaries are still used in parts of Bavaria, and they are worn on the belts of some Carmelite nuns, but the original form of the devotion in terms of its mysteries and visualizations has mostly been lost. The majority of six-decade rosaries on the market today are so-called Lourdes rosaries because the statue of Our Lady of Lourdes holds a rosary with six decades. These are oversize "wall" rosaries meant not for use in praying but rather for display.

A story grew up around the Lourdes rosary that, when Bernadette first prayed the rosary with the apparition, she reached the end of her prayers to find that Our Lady still had one decade of her rosary left to pray. "What are those beads for?" Bernadette asked, and the Lady replied, "Those beads are for the dead." The story does not appear in any existing record of the apparitions and may therefore be apocryphal. It is just as likely that the sculptor, Joseph Fabisch, gave the statue a six-decade rosary because such rosaries were still in use among rural peasants in nineteenth-century France. In that case, they would typically have used the extra decade to pray for their beloved dead.

For more information on the Corone, see Herbert Thurston's article "The So-called Brigittine Rosary" in *The Month*, no. 458 (August 1902), pp. 189–203. For a manual explaining one method originally for praying the Corone, read *The Rosarie of Our Ladie. Otherwise Called Our Ladies Psalter With Other Godlie Exercises Mentioned in the Preface*, by Thomas Worthington (originally published in Antwerp in 1600, now available in facsimile edition through Early English Books Online).

157 **Even today, psychics and mediums:** A notable example is the psychic medium John Edwards. In his book *Practical Praying: Using the Rosary to Enhance Your Life* (New York: Princess Books, 2005), Edwards describes his ritual one hour before going onstage to offer readings for audiences:

> Alone in my hotel room, I pick up my Rosary and silently begin to pray. I'm praying this decade for the audience to learn that their loved ones are still with them . . . I'm praying this decade for me to be a clear receiver for them tonight . . . I'm praying this decade for the energies to communicate with me in ways I will understand.
>
> The beads slip through my fingers as I pray with intention—envisioning that I'll be the best teacher I can possibly be when I step into the spotlight and begin taking questions.
>
> When I'm finished—it usually takes me about 30 minutes—I'm centered, focused, and tuned in to the Other Side. I'm ready to go to work.
>
> Using a Rosary to pray is a ritual I've performed before every reading, seminar, or group session in my 20 years as a psychic medium (pp. 1–2).

A Sword in Our Hearts

160 **Our Lady of Sorrows was a well-known title:** General information on Our Lady of Sorrows is obtainable online and through books on Mar-

ian iconography. For an extensive collection of prayers and rituals related to her, consult *Behold Thy Mother: A Collection of Devotions Chiefly in Honor of Our Lady of Sorrows, Compiled by the Servite Fathers* (available from www.JoyfulCatholic.com).

The Boy Drawer

170 **I received a call:** *New York Times* "Beliefs" columnist Mark Oppenheimer eventually wrote an entire book about the rise and fall of Eido Tai Shimano Roshi. See *The Zen Predator of the Upper East Side* (Washington, D.C.: The Atlantic Books, 2013). Described as "a cautionary tale of the dark side of Zen in America," its chronology of events ends before the reconciliation meeting described in this chapter.

Faster Than the Speed of Life

179 **But there is a case to be made:** The title of a popular online game—*1830: Railroads & Robber Barons*—confirms the link between that date and the economic expansionism (often predatory) that laid hold of Western economies in the mid-nineteenth century. The *Wikipedia* entry for the game describes it as follows:

> The goal of the game is to maximize personal wealth before the game ends, whether by nurturing a railroad company to increase its stock value, gutting it and running with the money, successful stock trading or arranging for another player to go bankrupt. Buying, trading and speculating on the stock market is often where 1830 is won or lost.
>
> A game is finished when the bank runs out of money or any player goes bankrupt, with the player with the greatest personal wealth winning.

Ashes, Ashes, We All Fall Down

182 **In the school yard children link hands:** Eithne Wilkins devotes an entire chapter of *The Rose-Garden Game* to the *ludus puerorum* (child's play) aspect of the rosary, a Latin term used to describe both the games of childhood and the proper "spirit of spontaneous play" that is necessary to complete the transformational processes of alchemy. She writes:

Play is the pure creative condition. That is why in the Book of Proverbs, where Wisdom says she was "set up from everlasting, from the beginning, or ever the earth was," she also says that she was present at the creation of the universe:

I was with him [God] as the master-craftsman, delighting him day after day, playing always in his presence, playing on the surface of his earth and delighting in frequenting with the children of men.

The affinity with play manifests itself in a very familiar childish example, that of the singing-game, Ring-a-ring o' roses. Whether the words were ever "ring-a-ring a rosary" will probably remain undiscoverable, but it is not at all far-fetched to suppose that they may have been, since the corresponding German game, with almost the same tune, has these words: Ringel-ringel Rosenkrantz. (p. 81)

Our Only Hope

185 **But don't try to tell us that alternative forms:** In his book *The Long Emergency: Surviving the End of Oil, Climate Change, and Other Converging Catastrophes of the Twenty-first Century* (New York: Grove Press, 2005), James Howard Kunstler offers a convincing argument that most aspects of modern civilization rest atop a platform of cheap, easily available petroleum—an essential chemical component of myriad products and technological processes that cannot be replaced with alternative forms of energy. Kunstler uses the term *techno-narcissism* to describe the belief that technology can solve all problems.

185 **Only then was he finally able:** Wilson chronicles his descent into alcoholism and suicidal depression, and his eventual recovery, in Chapter 1 of *Alcoholics Anonymous*: "Bill's Story."

Pray for Us Sinners

188 **"What is the essence of our own morality":** *The End of the Wild*, by the late Stephen M. Meyer (Cambridge, MA: MIT Press, 2006), provides a concise but sobering portrait of "human selection"—the idea that human activity has now replaced natural selection as the driving force of evolution, resulting in drastic, sudden declines in our planet's biodiversity.

Back to the Forest

190 **The oldest written story:** Of the many translations available today, Stephen Mitchell's *Gilgamesh: A New English Version* (New York: Free Press, 2006) is the best—at once accessible to the modern reader and evocative of the primeval beauty and grandeur of the original epic.

191 **Even some of the most sincere:** Consider Pope Francis's recent encyclical *On Care for Our Common Home: The Encyclical Letter Laudato Si'* (Mahwah, NJ: Paulist Press, 2015). In its response to the encyclical, the editors of *Nature* wrote:

> Alas, [the Pope] remained silent on issues of contraception. With a world population heading towards a possible 10 billion, the importance of family planning is clear. The Vatican has been brave on climate change. If it is serious about the fate of the planet and the welfare of its inhabitants, then it must be braver still on the issue of contraception.

See "Hope from the Pope" in *Nature* 522, no. 391 (June 25, 2015).

191 **In 2003, what was then the largest:** The Northeast blackout of August 14, 2003, was, at that time, the second largest power outage in world history. Over 55 million people lost electricity when a software malfunction caused a failure in the alert system at FirstEnergy Corporation in Akron, Ohio. Because operators remained unaware that transmission lines had become overloaded as a result of physical contact with one pine tree in Walton Hills, Ohio, what should have been a local blackout became the collapse of the entire electric grid.

Expect a Miracle

202 **What few people know today:** For an unfiltered account of the Apparition of the Miraculous Medal, see *Catherine Labouré and the Modern Apparitions of Our Lady*, by Abbé Omer Englebert, translated by Alastair Guinan (New York: Kenedy, 1959). What follows is a complete account of the initial apparition, in Catherine's own words, written in 1830 at the request of her confessor, Monsieur Aladel:

> I dressed quickly and joined the child. I followed after him. He went on my left, and from him came forth rays of light. To my

great astonishment lights were shining brightly all along our way. But my astonishment increased when, as we approached the chapel, the door opened at a slight touch of the child's finger.

My amazement was at its height as I then beheld all the candles and torches in the chapel lit in a way that reminded me of midnight Mass. However, I saw no sign of the Blessed Virgin.

The child led me into the sanctuary to the side of the chaplain's chair (on the Gospel side). Here I knelt down while the child remained standing. All this while I was looking to see whether the Sisters on watch would pass through the sanctuary.

Then a moment later the child said: "Here is the Blessed Virgin; here she is!"

I heard the rustling of a silken robe coming from the side of the sanctuary. The "Lady" bowed before the tabernacle, and then she seated herself in [the Chaplain's] chair . . .

(Seeing that) I did not know how to behave, the Child spoke to me again: "It is the Blessed Virgin!" I am not able to say why, but it still seemed to me that it was not she whom I saw. It was then that the voice of the child changed and took on the deeper tones of a man's voice. He spoke again, strongly, repeating the words for a third time.

At this moment I rushed forward and knelt before the Blessed Virgin with my hands on her knees. I cannot express what I felt, but I am sure that this was the happiest moment of my life.

Catherine never revealed what the Lady told her at the time of the first apparition, although from her account they must have spent more than two hours together.

The Long Story

210 **Christine Desdemaines-Hugon was a former painter**: For an eye-opening tour through the art of the Upper Paleolithic, read *Stepping-Stones: A Journey Through the Ice Age Caves of the Dordogne*. For those who wish to experience cave art in person, tours can be booked through her website: http://www.caveconnection.fr/.

217 **Within walking distance from the chapel:** Discovered in 1921, when the owner of the property disturbed a pile of stones in which some animals had made a nest, La Grotte des Merveilles (the Grotto of Won-

ders) is one of several painted caves in Quercy, a region of France occupied by hominids for over 300,000 years.

221 **That's when Clark saw a sign:** For a spectacular virtual tour of Le Site Madeleine, available in six languages, visit: http://www.la-madeleine-perigord.com/?lang=en.

The Column of Saints

225 **When you hear of a column:** Many of the chapters that follow combine two or more of Our Lady's messages on a related theme. For the complete messages of Our Lady of Woodstock in chronological order, visit the section "Our Lady Speaks" at wayoftherose.org.

Bibliography

Addiction and Recovery

Alcoholics Anonymous: The Story of How Many Thousands of Men and Women Have Recovered from Alcoholism. 4th ed. New York: Alcoholics Anonymous World Services, 2001.

Cheever, Susan. *My Name Is Bill: Bill Wilson—His Life and the Creation of Alcoholics Anonymous*. New York: Simon & Schuster, 2004.

Kurtz, Ernest. *Not-God: A History of Alcoholics Anonymous*. Center City, MN: Hazelden, 1979.

LaChance, Albert J. *Cultural Addiction: The Greenspirit Guide to Recovery*. Berkeley, CA: North Atlantic Books, 1991.

McQ., Joe. *The Steps We Took*. Atlanta, GA: August House Publishers, 1990.

"Pass It On": The Story of Bill Wilson and How the AA Message Reached the World. New York: Alcoholics Anonymous World Services, 1984.

Shapiro, Rami. *Recovery: The Twelve Steps as Spiritual Practice*. Woodstock, VT: Skylight Paths, 2009.

Twelve Steps and Twelve Traditions. New York: Alcoholics Anonymous World Services, 1981.

Climate Change, Humanity, and the Environment

Archer, David. *The Long Thaw: How Humans Are Changing the Next 100,000 Years of Earth's Climate*. Princeton, NJ: Princeton University Press, 2009.

Berry, Thomas. *The Dream of the Earth*. San Francisco: Sierra Club Books, 1988.

Ceballos, Gerardo, Paul R. Erhlich, and Rodolfo Dirzo. "Biological Annihilation via the Ongoing Sixth Mass Extinction Signaled by Vertebrate Population Losses and Declines." *Proceedings of the National Academy of Sciences*, July 25, 2017.

Craven, Greg. *What's the Worst That Could Happen? A Rational Response to the Climate Change Debate*. New York: Penguin, 2009.

Diamond, Jared. *Collapse: How Societies Choose to Fail or Succeed*. New York: Viking, 2005.

———. *Guns, Germs, and Steel: The Fates of Human Societies*. New York: Norton, 1997.

Draffan, George, and Derek Jensen. *Strangely Like War: The Global Assault on Forests*. White River Junction, VT: Chelsea Green Publishing, 2003.

Friends of the Earth. *The Stockholm Conference: Only One Earth*. London: Earth Island Limited, 1972.

Fukuoka, Masanobu. *The One-Straw Revolution*. New York: New York Review of Books, 1978.

Ghosh, Amitav. *The Great Derangement: Climate Change and the Unthinkable*. Chicago: University of Chicago Press, 2016.

Hartmann, Thom. *The Last Hours of Ancient Sunlight: The Fate of the World and What We Can Do Before It's Too Late*. New York: Three Rivers Press, 1998.

Jensen, Derrick. *Dreams*. New York: Seven Stories Press, 2011.

———. *Endgame, Vol. I: The Problem of Civilization* and *Endgame, Vol. II: Resistance*. New York: Seven Stories Press, 2006.

———. *A Language Older Than Words*. New York: Context Books, 2000.

———. *The Myth of Human Supremacy*. New York: Seven Stories Press, 2016.

Keith, Lierre. *The Vegetarian Myth: Food, Justice, and Sustainability*. Crescent City, CA: Flashpoint Press, 2009.

Korten, David C. *The Great Turning: From Empire to Earth Community*. San Francisco: Berrett-Koehler, 2006.

Kunstler, James Howard. *The Long Emergency: Surviving the End of Oil, Climate Change, and Other Converging Catastrophes of the Twenty-first Century*. New York: Grove Press, 2005.

———. *Too Much Magic: Wishful Thinking, Technology, and the Fate of the Nation*. New York: Grove Press, 2013.

Lanier, Jaron. *You Are Not a Gadget: A Manifesto*. New York: Vintage, 2010.

Las Casas, Bartolomé de. *A Short Account of the Destruction of the Indies*. Translated by Nigel Griffen. London: Penguin, 1999.

Lopez, Antonia. *The Media Ecosystem: What Ecology Can Teach Us about Responsible Media Practice*. Berkeley, CA: Evolver Editions, 2012.

Lovelock, James. *The Revenge of Gaia*. London: Penguin, 2007.

Meyer, Stephen M. *The End of the Wild*. Cambridge, MA: MIT Press, 2006.

Monbiot, George. *Feral: Rewilding the Land, the Sea, and Human Life*. Chicago: University of Chicago Press, 2014.

Quinn, Daniel. *Ishmael: An Adventure of the Mind and Spirit*. New York: Bantam, 1992.

Schell, Jonathan. *The Fate of the Earth*. New York: Knopf, 1982.

Scranton, Roy. *Learning to Die in the Anthropocene: Reflections on the End of Civilization*. San Francisco: City Lights Books, 2015.

Stanley, John, et al., eds. *A Buddhist Response to the Climate Emergency*. Boston: Wisdom Publications, 2009.

Weisman, Alan. *Countdown*. New York: Little, Brown, 2013.

———. *The World Without Us*. New York: St. Martin's Press, 2007.

Wessels, Tom. *The Myth of Progress: Toward a Sustainable Future*. Burlington: University of Vermont Press, 2006.

Wilson, E. O. *The Creation: An Appeal to Save Life on Earth*. New York: Norton, 2006.

———. *Half-Earth: Our Planet's Fight for Life*. New York: Liveright, 2016.

The Goddess in History, Art, and Legend

Abbot, Raylene. *A Mystic's Journey to the Sacred Sites of France*. Ramajon: Bikeapelli Press, 2010.

Apostolos-Cappadona, Diane. *Dictionary of Women in Religious Art*. New York: Oxford University Press, 1998.

Apuleius. *The Golden Ass*. Translated by W. Adlington. Cambridge, MA: Harvard University Press, 1977.

Austen, Hallie Iglehart. *The Heart of the Goddess: Art, Myth and Meditations of the World's Sacred Feminine*. Rhinebeck, NY: Monkfish Publishing, 2018.

Baring, Anne, and Jules Cashford. *The Myth of the Goddess: Evolution of an Image*. London: Penguin Arkana, 1991.

Begg, Ean. *The Cult of the Black Virgin*. London: Arkana, 1985.

Bolen, Jean Shinoda. *Crossing to Avalon*. New York: HarperCollins, 1994.

Browne, Sylvia. *Mother God: The Feminine Principle to Our Creator*. Carlsbad, CA: Hay House, 2004.

Burstein, Dan, and Arne J. De Keijzer, eds. *Secrets of Mary Magdalene: The Untold Story of History's Most Misunderstood Woman*. Cambridge, MA: Squibnocket Partners, 2006.

Ehrman, Bart D. *Lost Scriptures: Books That Did Not Make It into the New Testament*. Oxford: Oxford University Press, 2003.

Frazer, James George. *The Golden Bough: A Study in Magic and Religion*. Oxford: Oxford University Press, 1994.

Gadon, Elinor W. *The Once and Future Goddess: A Sweeping Visual Chroni-*

cle of the Sacred Female and Her Reemergence in the Cultural Mythology of Our Time. New York: Harper & Row, 1989.

George, Demetra. *Mysteries of the Dark Moon: The Healing Power of the Dark Goddess*. New York: HarperOne, 1992.

Gimbutas, Marija. *Civilization of the Goddess: The World of Old Europe*. San Francisco: HarperSanFrancisco, 1991.

Godwin, Joscelyn, trans. *The Chemical Wedding of Christian Rosenkreutz*. Grand Rapids, MI: Phanes Press, 1991.

Graves, Robert. *Mammon and the Black Goddess*. New York: Doubleday, 1965.

Hani, Jean. *The Black Virgin: A Marian Mystery*. Translated by Robert Proctor. San Rafael, CA: Sophia Perennis, 2007.

Harding, Elizabeth U. *Kali: The Black Goddess of Dakshineswar*. York Beach, ME: Red Wheel Weiser, 1993.

Hixon, Lex. *Mother of the Buddhas: Meditation on the Prajanparamita Sutra*. Wheaton, IL: Quest Books, 1993.

———. *Mother of the Universe: Visions of the Goddess and Tantric Hymns of Enlightenment*. Wheaton, IL: Quest Books, 1994.

Johnson, Buffie. *Lady of the Beasts: Ancient Images of the Goddess and Her Sacred Animals*. San Francisco: HarperSanFrancisco, 1988.

Leloup, Jean-Yves. *The Gospel of Mary Magdalene*. Translated by Joseph Rowe. Rochester, VT: Inner Traditions, 2002.

———. *The Sacred Embrace of Jesus and Mary: The Sexual Mystery at the Heart of the Christian Tradition*. Rochester, VT: Inner Traditions, 2005.

Markale, Jean. *Cathedral of the Black Madonna: The Druids and the Mysteries of Chartres*. Rochester, VT: Inner Traditions, 1988.

Matthews, Caitlin. *Sophia: Goddess of Wisdom, Bride of God*. Wheaton, IL: Quest Books, 2001.

McDaniel, June. *Offering Flowers, Feeding Skulls: Popular Goddess Worship in West Bengal*. New York: Oxford University Press, 2004.

McLean, Malcolm. *Devoted to the Goddess: The Life and Work of Ramprasad*. Albany: State University of New York Press, 1998.

Meredith, Jane. *Journey to the Dark Goddess: How to Return to Your Soul*. Winchester, UK: Moon Books, 2012.

Mookerjee, Ajit. *Kali: The Feminine Force*. Rochester, VT: Destiny Books, 1988.

Pagels, Elaine. *Adam, Eve, and the Serpent*. New York: Vintage, 1988.

Perera, Sylvia Brinton. *Descent to the Goddess: A Way of Initiation for Women*. Toronto: Inner City Books, 1981.

Picknett, Lynn. *Mary Magdalene: Christianity's Hidden Goddess*. New York: Carroll & Graf, 2003.

Raff, Jeffrey. *The Wedding of Sophia: The Divine Feminine in Psychoidal Alchemy*. York, ME: Red Wheel Weiser, 2003.

Ralls, Karen. *Mary Magdalene: Her History and Myths Revealed*. New York: Shelter Harbor Press, 2013.

Robinson, James M., ed. *The Nag Hammadi Library*. San Francisco: HarperSanFrancisco, 1990.

Rollin, Tracey. *Santa Muerta: The History, Rituals, and Magic of Our Lady of the Holy Death*. Newburyport, MA: Red Wheel Weiser, 2017.

Roob, Alexander. *Alchemy & Mysticism*. Cologne: Taschen, 2018.

Schipflinger, Thomas. *Sophia-Maria: A Holistic Vision of Creation*. Translated by James Morgante. York Beach, ME: Red Wheel Weiser, 1998.

Sjoo, Monica, and Barbara Mor. *The Great Cosmic Mother: Rediscovering the Religion of the Earth*. San Francisco: HarperSanFrancisco, 1987.

Spretnak, Charlene. *Lost Goddesses of Early Greece*. Boston: Beacon Press, 1978.

Starbird, Margaret. *The Woman with the Alabaster Jar: Mary Magdalene and the Holy Grail*. Rochester, VT: Bear, 1993.

Starhawk. *Dreaming the Dark: Magic, Sex & Politics*. Boston: Beacon Press, 1982.

Steiner, Rudolf. *Isis, Mary, Sophia: Her Mission and Ours*. Great Barrington, MA: Steiner Books, 2003.

Von Franz, Marie-Louise. *The Cat: A Tale of Female Redemption*. Toronto: Inner City Books, 1999.

Walker, Barbara G. *The Woman's Encyclopedia of Myths and Secrets*. San Francisco: Harper & Row, 1983.

Wikman, Monika. *Pregnant Darkness: Alchemy and the Rebirth of Consciousness*. York Beach, ME: Red Wheel Weiser, 2004.

Wolkstein, Diane, and Samuel Noah Kramer. *Inanna, Queen of Heaven and Earth: Her Stories and Hymns from Sumer*. New York: Harper & Row, 1983.

Woodman, Marian. *The Pregnant Virgin: A Process of Psychological Transformation*. Toronto: Inner City Books, 1985.

Marian Apparitions

Alday, Salvador Carrillo. *The Theological Message of Guadalupe*. New York: Society of St. Paul/Alba House, 2010.

Blackbourn, David. *Marpingen: Apparitions of the Virgin Mary in Nineteenth-Century Germany*. New York: Knopf, 1994.

Connell, Janice T. *Queen of the Cosmos: Interviews with the Visionaries of Medjugorje*. Orleans, MA: Paraclete Press, 1990.

———. *Meetings with Mary: Visions of the Blessed Mother*. New York: Ballantine, 1995.

Donofrio, Beverly. *Looking for Mary: (Or the Blessed Mother and Me)*. New York: Viking, 2000.

Elizondo, Virgil. *Guadalupe: Mother of the New Creation*. Maryknoll, NY: Orbis Books, 1997.

Englebert, Omer. *Catherine Labouré and the Modern Apparitions of Our Lady*. Translated by Alastair Guinan. New York: Kenedy, 1959.

Ilibagiza, Immaculée. *Left to Tell: Discovering God Amidst the Rwandan Holocaust*. Carlsbad, CA: Hay House, 2006.

———. *Our Lady of Kibeho: Mary Speaks to the World from the Heart of Africa*. Carlsbad, CA: Hay House, 2008.

Laurentin, René. *Bernadette Speaks: A Life of Saint Bernadette Soubirous in Her Own Words*. Translated by John W. Lynch. Boston: Pauline Books & Media, 2000.

Marchi, John de. *The True Story of Fatima: A Complete Account of the Fatima Apparitions*. Constable, NY: Fatima Center, 1947.

Mini, John. *The Aztec Virgin: The Secret Mystical Tradition of Our Lady of Guadalupe*. Sausalito, CA: Trans-Hyperborean Institute of Science, 2000.

O'Connor, Edward D. *Marian Apparitions Today: Why So Many?* Santa Barbara, CA: Queenship Publishing, 1996.

Rooney, Lucy, and Robert Faricy. *Medjugorje Up Close: Mary Speaks to the World*. New York: Franciscan Herald Books, 1985.

Solimeo, Luiz Sergio. *Fatima: A Message More Urgent Than Ever*. Spring Grove, PA: American Society for the Defense of Tradition, Family and Property, 2017.

Werfel, Franz. *The Song of Bernadette*. New York: Viking, 1942.

Marian Devotion

Ash, Geoffrey. *The Virgin*. London: Routledge & Kegan, 1976.

Brown, Rachel Fulton. *Mary & the Art of Prayer: The Hours of the Virgin in Medieval Christian Life and Thought*. New York: Columbia University Press, 2018.

Brown, Raphael. *The Life of Mary as Seen by the Mystics*. Charlotte, NC: TAN Books, 1951.

Bull, Marcus. *The Miracles of Our Lady of Rocamadour: Analysis and Translation*. Woodbridge, UK: Boydell Press, 1999.

Cragon, Julie Dortch. *Visiting Mary: Her U.S. Shrines and Their Graces*. Cincinnati, OH: Franciscan Media, 2014.

De Montfort, Louis Mary. *True Devotion to Mary with Preparation for Total Consecration*. Translated by Frederick William Faber. Charlotte, NC: TAN Books, 2010.

Estés, Clarissa Pinkola. *Untie the Strong Woman: Blessed Mother's Immaculate Love for the Wild Soul*. Boulder, CO: Sounds True, 2011.

Finucane, Ronald C. *Miracles & Pilgrims: Popular Beliefs in Medieval England*. Guildford, UK: Aldine Press, 1977.

Gaventa, Beverly Roberts, and Cynthia L. Rigby, eds. *Blessed One: Protestant Perspectives on Mary*. Louisville, KY: Westminster John Knox Press, 2002.

Gold, Penny Schine. *The Lady & the Virgin: Image, Attitude, and Experience in Twelfth-century France*. Chicago: University of Chicago Press, 1985.

Lamberty, Manetta. *The Woman in Orbit: Mary's Feasts Every Day Everywhere*. Chicago: Lamberty, 1966.

Liguori, Alphonsus. *Hail Holy Queen: An Explanation of the Salve Regina*. Rockford, IL: TAN Books, 1995.

Mary of Agreda. *The Mystical City of God: The Divine History and Life of the Virgin Mother of God*. Translated by Fiscar Marison. Rockford, IL: TAN Books, 1949.

Nastorg, P. Clement. *Rocamadour: Admire, Contemplate, Pray*. Translated by Oliver Todd. Strasbourg: Editions du Signe, 2006.

Ruffin, C. Bernard. *Padre Pio: The True Story*. Huntingdon, IN: Our Sunday Visitor Books, 1991.

Shapiro, Rami. *The Love of Eternal Wisdom: A Revisioning of Saint Louis DeMontfort's Contemplation on Divine Wisdom*. Litchfield, CT: Wisdom House, 2011.

Spretnak, Charlene. *Missing Mary: The Queen of Heaven and Her Reemergence in the Modern Church*. New York: Palgrave Macmillan, 2004.

Storey, G. William, ed. *A Book of Marian Prayers: A Compilation of Marian Devotions from the Second to the Twenty-first Century*. Chicago: Loyola Press, 2011.

Underhill, Evelyn. *The Miracles of Our Lady Saint Mary: Brought Out of Diverse Tongues and Newly Set Forth in English*. New York: Dutton, 1906.

Warner, Marina. *Alone of All Her Sex: The Myth and the Cult of the Virgin Mary*. New York: Vintage, 1983.

The Natural World

Andrews, Ted. *Animal-Speak: The Spiritual and Magical Powers of Creatures Great & Small*. St. Paul, MN: Llewellyn Publications, 1997.

Buhner, Stephen Harrod. *The Lost Language of Plants*. White River Junction, VT: Chelsea Green, 2002.

Cashford, Jules. *The Moon: Myth and Image*. New York: Four Walls Eight Windows, 2003.

Foster, Charles. *Being a Beast: Adventures Across the Species Divide*. New York: Metropolitan Books, 2016.

Freinkel, Susan. *American Chestnut: The Life, Death, and Rebirth of a Perfect Tree*. Berkeley: University of California Press, 2007.

Harrison, Robert Pogue. *Forests: The Shadow of Civilization*. Chicago: University of Chicago Press, 1992.

Haskell, David George. *The Songs of Trees: Stories from Nature's Great Connectors*. New York: Viking, 2017.

Heinrich, Bernd. *Life Everlasting: The Animal Way of Death*. New York: Houghton Mifflin Harcourt, 2012.

Logan, William Bryant. *Dirt: The Ecstatic Skin of the Earth*. New York: Norton, 1995.

Nicholls, Steve. *Paradise Found: Nature in America at the Time of Discovery*. Chicago: University of Chicago Press, 2009.

Pollan, Michael. *The Botany of Desire: A Plant's-Eye View of the World*. New York: Random House, 2002.

Pyle, Robert. *How to Grow Roses*. West Grove, PA: Conard and Jones, 1923.

Safer, Shiila. *Intimacy with Trees*. Wimberley, TX: 2nd Tier Publishing, 2015.

Stewart, George R. *Earth Abides*. New York: Del Rey, 1976.

Taylor, Bron. *Dark Green Religion: Nature Spirituality and the Planetary Future*. Berkeley: University of California Press, 2010.

Paleoanthropology and History

Barstow, Anne Llewellyn. *Witchcraze: Our Legacy of Violence Against Women*. New York: HarperCollins, 1994.

Brown, Cynthia Stokes. *Big History: From the Big Bang to the Present*. New York: Norton, 2007.

Curtis, Gregory. *The Cave Painters: Probing the Mysteries of the World's First Artists*. New York: Anchor, 2006.

Dashu, Max. *Witches and Pagans: Women in European Folk Religion 700–1100*. Richmond, CA: Veleda Press, 2016.

Desdemaines-Hugon, Christine. *Stepping-Stones: A Journey Through the Ice Age Caves of the Dordogne*. New Haven: Yale University Press, 2010.

Eisler, Riane. *The Chalice and the Blade: Our History, Our Future*. New York: HarperCollins, 1988.

Fortey, Richard. *Life: A Natural History of the First Four Billion Years of Life on Earth*. New York: Knopf, 1999.

Francis. *On Care for Our Common Home: The Encyclical Letter Laudato Si'*. Mahwah, NJ: Paulist Press, 2015.

Goddio, Franck, and David Fabre. *Osiris: Egypt's Sunken Mysteries*. Paris: Flammarion, 2015.

Grahn, Judy. *Blood, Bread, and Roses: How Menstruation Created the World*. Boston: Beacon Press, 1993.

Lévi-Strauss, Claude. *Myth and Meaning: Cracking the Code of Culture*. New York: Schocken, 1979.

Lewis-Williams, David. *The Mind in the Cave: Consciousness and the Origins of Art*. London: Thames & Hudson, 2002.

MacGregor, Neil. *A History of the World in 100 Objects*. New York: Viking, 2010.

McKibben, Bill, ed. *American Earth: Environmental Writing Since Thoreau*. New York: Library of America, 2008.

Mitchell, Stephen. *Gilgamesh: A New English Version*. New York: Free Press, 2006.

Mithen, Steven. *After the Ice: A Global Human History 20,000–5,000 B.C.* Cambridge: Harvard University Press, 2003.

O'Hara, Kieran D. *Cave Art and Climate Change*. Bloomington, IN: Archway, 2014.

Ong, Walter J. *Orality and Literacy: The Technologizing of the Word*. New York: Routledge, 2002.

Quammen, David. *The Tangled Tree: A Radical New History of Life*. New York: Simon & Schuster, 2018.

Renfrew, Colin. *Prehistory: The Making of the Human Mind*. New York: Modern Library, 2007.

Sale, Kirkpatrick. *After Eden: The Evolution of Human Domination*. Durham, NC: Duke University Press, 2006.

Schlain, Leonard. *The Alphabet Versus the Goddess: The Conflict Between Word and Image*. New York: Penguin, 1998.

Silverman, David P., ed. *Ancient Egypt*. New York: Oxford University Press, 1997.

Smail, Daniel Lord. *On Deep History and the Brain*. Berkeley: University of California Press, 2007.

Snyder, Gary. *Earth House Hold: Technical Notes & Queries to Fellow Dharma Revolutionaries*. New York: New Directions, 1969.

Tarnas, Richard. *Cosmos and Psyche: Intimations of a New World View*. New York: Penguin, 2006.

Trevor-Roper, H. R. *The European Witch Craze of the Sixteenth and Seventeenth Centuries*. New York: Harper & Row, 1969.

The Rosary and Bead Practices

Ayo, Nicholas. *The Hail Mary: A Verbal Icon of Mary*. Notre Dame, IN: University of Notre Dame Press, 1994.

Boyer, Mark G. *Reflections on the Mysteries of the Rosary*. Collegeville, MN: Liturgical Press, 2005.

Bryan, David Burton. *A Western Way of Meditation: The Rosary Revisited*. Chicago: Loyola University Press, 1991.

De Montfort, Louis Mary. *The Secret of the Rosary*. Translated by Mary Barbour. Charlotte, NC: TAN Books, 1987.

Dicharry, Warren. *Praying the Rosary*. Collegeville, MN: Liturgical Press, 1998.

Edwards, Gail Faith. *Through the Wild Heart of Mary: Teachings of the 20 Mysteries of the Rosary and the Herbs and Foods Associated with Them*. Athens, ME: Rosina Publishing, 2009.

Edwards, John. *Practical Praying: Using the Rosary to Enhance Your Life*. New York: Princess Books, 2005.

Fulton, Rachel. "The Virgin in the Garden, or Why Flowers Make Better Prayers." *Spiritus: A Journal of Christian Spirituality* 4, no. 1 (Spring 2004).

Greer, John Michael, and Clare Vaughn. *Pagan Prayer Beads: Magic and Meditation with Pagan Rosaries*. San Francisco: Weiser Books, 2007.

Gribble, Richard. *The History and Devotion of the Rosary*. Huntington, IN: Our Sunday Visitor Publishing, 1992.

Habig, Marion A. *The Franciscan Crown*. New York: Franciscan Herald Press, 1976.

Hoffner, Gloria Brady, and Helen Hoffner. *The Rosary Collector's Guide*. Atglen, PA: Schiffer Publishing, 2013.

Ilibagiza, Immaculée. *The Rosary: The Prayer That Saved My Life*. Carlsbad, CA: Hay House, 2013.

Jansen, Gary. *The Rosary: A Journey to the Beloved*. New York: Madison Park Press, 2006.

Johnson, Kevin Orlin. *Rosary: Mysteries, Meditations, and the Telling of the Beads*. Dallas: Pangaeus Press, 1996.

Lacey, Charles. *Rosary Novenas to Our Lady*. Chicago: ACTA Publications, 2003.

Laning, Chris. *Bedes Byddyng: Medieval Rosaries & Paternoster Beads*. Milpitas, CA: Society for Creative Anachronism, 2007.

Lelen, J. M. *Pray the Rosary for Rosary Novenas, Family Rosary, Private Recitation, First Five Saturdays*. Totowa, NJ: Catholic Book Publishing, 1953.

Miller, John D. *Beads & Prayers: The Rosary in History & Devotion*. London: Burns & Oates, 2002.

Staal, Frits. *Ritual and Mantras: Rules Without Meaning*. New York: North-Holland, 1986.

Sweeney, Jon M. *Praying with Our Hands: 21 Practices of Embodied Prayer from the World's Spiritual Traditions*. Woodstock, VT: Skylight Paths, 2000.

Thurston, Herbert. "The So-called Brigittine Rosary." *The Month*, no. 458 (August 1902).

———. "Alan de Rupe and His Indulgence of 60,000 Years." *The Month*, no. 459 (September 1902).

Weber, Christin Lore. *Circle of Mysteries: The Woman's Rosary Book*. St. Paul, MN: Yes International, 1995.

Wilkins, Eithne. *The Rose-Garden Game: A Tradition of Beads and Flowers*. New York: Herder and Herder, 1969.

Willam, Franz Michel. *The Rosary: Its History and Meaning*. Translated by Edwin Kaiser. New York: Christ the King Library, 1952.

Wills, Garry. *The Rosary*. New York: Viking, 2005.

Winston-Allen, Anne. *Stories of the Rose: The Making of the Rosary in the Middle Ages*. University Park: Pennsylvania State University Press, 1997.

Worthington, Thomas. *The Rosarie of Our Ladie: Otherwise Called Our Ladies Psalter With Other Godlie Exercises Mentioned in the Preface*. Antwerp: n.p., 1600; facsimile edition, Early English Books Online.

ABOUT THE AUTHORS

Clark Strand and Perdita Finn are co-founders of The Way of the Rose, an inclusive fellowship of rosary friends dedicated to the Earth and to the Lady "by any name we wish to call Her." Strand is the author of numerous books and articles on spiritual practices, including *Seeds from a Birch Tree: Writing Haiku and the Spiritual Journey* and *Waking Up to the Dark: Ancient Wisdom for a Sleepless Age.* Finn is a children's book author and former high school teacher. They live with their family in the Catskill Mountains.

wayoftherose.org
Find The Way of the Rose on Facebook

ABOUT THE ILLUSTRATOR

Will Lytle (aka Thorneater Comics) is an artist and illustrator whose work is deeply influenced by the natural environment of his native Catskill Mountains and the magic long associated with that region in legend and folklore. His murals and art installations have appeared in a variety of public and commercial venues—from New York to Paris.

ABOUT THE TYPE

This book was set in Electra, a typeface designed for Linotype by W. A. Dwiggins, the renowned type designer (1880–1956). Electra is a fluid typeface, avoiding the contrasts of thick and thin strokes that are prevalent in most modern typefaces.